JAPANTHEM

JAPANTHEM

COUNTER-CULTURAL EXPERIENCES, CROSS-CULTURAL REMIXES

Jillian Marshall

with an introduction by
Steven F. Pond

THREE ROOMS PRESS
New York, NY

Japanthem:
Counter-Cultural Experiences, Cross-Cultural Remixes
BY Jillian Marshall

This is a work of creative nonfiction. The events are portrayed to the best of the author's memory. Some parts of this book, including dialog, characters and their characteristics, locations and time, may not be entirely factual.

ISBN 978-1-953103-15-4 (trade paperback)
ISBN 978-1-953103-16-1 (Epub)
Library of Congress Control Number: 2021948044

TRP-094

First Edition
Pub Date: April 12, 2022

Nonfiction Adult
BISAC Coding:
MUS015000   Music / Ethnomusicology
TRV003050   Travel / Asia / East / Japan
BIO004000   Biography & Autobiography / Music
SOC008020   Social Science / Ethnic Studies / Asian Studies

COVER DESIGN AND BOOK DESIGN:
KG Design International: www.katgeorges.com

COVER IMAGE:
Two Kansai-Based DJs raging into the night in Matsuyama Prefecture.
Photo Copyright © Jillian Marshall

DISTRIBUTED IN THE U.S. AND INTERNATIONALLY BY:
Publishers Group West: www.pgw.com

Three Rooms Press
New York, NY
www.threeroomspress.com
info@threeroomspress.com

For Mayuko Ogawa

En (縁): a connection with a person or place, supported by synchronicity or coincidence; the stuff of destiny, but not destiny itself; a fatedness of path; karma, played out; an inexplicable nudge in some particular direction

Notes on the Text

All events in the following story are true, at least from the author's perspective.[1] *Names of people and places have been changed to protect anonymity. Japanese words are italicized.*

---

1   I'm reminded of a fabulous "ism": "There are three sides to every story—what he said, what she said, and the truth." As a scholar, you better believe I challenge notions of objectivity. In fact, my skepticism constituted pretty much the entire first chapter of my original dissertation.

CONTENTS

Introduction
by Steven F. Pond

ISN'T THIS AN ACADEMIC BOOK? IT doesn't exactly feel like one. Jillian Marshall puts plenty of distance between herself and The Academy. But she puts *no* distance between herself and her purposeful immersion in three musical scenes—the life, the experience, the processes of learning, of affinities, of hierarchies—of musicking in Japan. But hold on: if it's not an academic book, why is it so brimming with insights about the people in these three scenes and, crucially, about her own relationship to Japan and to the institution that made her work possible and necessary?

Reading her introduction, I sometimes boiled. She spends a fair amount of ink trashing the academy, or at least the culture of worry and pain that too often grad students find to be their lot. Who writes that kind of stuff and expects to find a tenure-track job inside some leafy campus? But since reading it, I've certainly spent some time contemplating grad student culture, and how we academics should be re-thinking our mission and our methods.

Yes, it *is* an academic book, even though Jill Marshall's writing is so utterly engaging it's easy to forget this. Her style reminds me of Molly Ivins at her most cutting and sarcastic

i

and breathtakingly honest. Her methodology and her self-reflective authorial stance remind me of John Miller Chernoff's *African Rhythm and African Sensibility* (University of Chicago Press, 1978). Or the "comedy of academic manners" of David Lodge's *The Campus Trilogy* novels.

An academic researcher's job description is made of two basic parts: learn about stuff and then share it. But that learning and that stuff can come from lots of motivations and can manifest in many ways. Ethnographers (usually anthropologists and ethnomusicologists) find themselves caught in an impossible nexus. It doesn't matter how sensitive and determined we are to avoid the lingering colonialist stench of examining a culture—people individual and collectivized, folks and their ways—as objects for study. Anthropologists might look through the lens of religion, or food, or clothing, or whatever we can fix on as an entry point to understanding. Ethnomusicologists use music: folks making it, hearing it, consuming it, using it in society. At bottom, though, the ethnography project is to learn about people other than ourselves, or learn about people similar to ourselves but *not* ourselves, and explain what we know about these folks to people who, we assume, know even less about them than we do. Or at least know different things about them than we do. And so, as long as the lens is trained on the people doing the music or eating the food and *not* on the one trying to learn about and then interpret them, that insipient colonialism is just there, hidden but breathing. Why do ethnography that way?

It's complicated. In my experience, it starts with curiosity, but almost immediately gets blended with love. Then, often, comes the over-thinking. Are my motives pure? Are my observations accurate? Are they objective? Am I advocating too much? Am I being respectful enough of my interlocutors? Underlying this is an earnest desire not to make the book or article about the author, which would be unacceptably hubristic.

But more than a few anthropologists and ethnomusicologists have noticed that the ethnographer always becomes part of the scene being studied, always interacts with it and so influences it, always is involved in power hierarchies and identities that form a part of any sub-culture. And inevitably, ethnography results in change in the ethnographer; you could even say ethnography at some level is "about" the ethnographer. Now, as an ethnographer you can recoil from this fact; you can allow a crack in the "fourth wall," to invoke film jargon for a moment, but keep it to only a crack, a hint of your self-awareness of your place in the tale. Or you can embrace it, laying bare your struggles and flashes of insight, of scrubbing for money or friendship or personal wisdom while loving, learning from, and sharing understanding with the people in the scene. Jill has chosen to walk into the frame of the movie, revealing herself as not only present, but a central character in her own story.

On the other hand, this is a *post-academic* book. Or maybe Jill has used this writing to exorcize that demon pressing on her chest. "Getting it right" for the academic types, or even her interlocutors, isn't such a clear-cut goal; its importance pales next to getting it out, as a process.

In the end, what draws together the traditionalist culture-bearers of Akita's annual *obon* festival and the middle-aged men stealthily watching AKB48, that girl-group phenomenon metastasizing across Japan and beyond, with Japan's underground noise-based electronica deejays? It's Jiru, the *gaijin* outsider and Lover of People.

Jill Marshall came to Cornell in 2011 to pursue a PhD in ethnomusicology (even though Cornell's program resists separating "ethno" from musicology). My own training is in ethnomusicology, even though most of my "fieldwork" is on the phone, and most of my writing deals with historical subjects. I didn't know how I could guide her, but agreed to chair her academic committee. My "guidance" mostly consisted of reassuring her that she was smart as hell and on a productive track. She didn't need me. But I'm grateful to be honored by our friendship and for being in a position to encourage her.

Read the book. And be ready to change. And I'm also looking at you, Academe.

Steven F. Pond
Ithaca, NY

Associate Professor, Cornell University; Author, *Head Hunters: The Making of Jazz's First Platinum Album*

JAPANTHEM

Toward a Public Intellectualism

AFTER FINALLY PUSHING "SEND" ON MY doctoral dissertation, I immediately packed up my apartment, cleaned it for
the next tenant, and drove a U-Haul to New York City to live
life, for the first time, as a non-academic. About six months
later, my diploma arrived in the mail after I had to re-submit
my dissertation due to a blank page in the final PDF, and I
promptly stuffed it in a chest where I keep old cards, photos,
and other mementos from the past. It wasn't until a few
months had passed that I took it out for a proper examination. Thick parchment, a reflective seal of the university,
excitingly formal calligraphic font, and signatures written in
fountain pen:

> *Be it Known that Jillian Marshall,*
> *having fulfilled in full the requirements*
> *for the degree of Doctor of Philosophy . . .*

—

ACADEMIA, FOR THOSE NOT INDOCTRINATED, IS the official term for the academic world: professors, graduate and
undergraduate students, and their interactions with libraries,
archives, campuses, conferences, and so forth.

Unlike in other graduate programs, those that undertake a PhD—short for Doctor of Philosophy—are told that "getting a job" means becoming a professor. It's essentially professor training school, particularly in the humanities and social sciences where the job market clout isn't as obviously transferrable as it is with the hard sciences. For instance, holding a PhD does not qualify one to teach in most public-school systems—a degree in education is required, and the years of teaching experience one gains during the course of their doctoral studies don't readily transfer. We "nonpractical humanities-types" are thus trained to understand and engage with the literature, research, and modes of thought in our respective fields; as an ethnomusicologist of Japan, my work is thus informed by anthropology, music performance and theory, and Asian Studies. The sheer breadth and depth of doctoral research—combined with the responsibilities to submit papers to conferences, conduct original research, and teach undergraduate classes—are what qualify the PhD student to become an expert on their topic of study, and therefore a professor.

The issue is that the training is circular, and perhaps, even incestuous. Given that professors train professors-to-be, academia's perspectives are at risk of becoming myopic: woefully uninformed by the "outside world," except as it's clinically observed during fieldwork. Plus, I dare say that the majority of those accepted into PhD programs—and certainly those that go on to full professorship—have limited, if any, experience in the nonacademic workforce. This isn't so much a reflection of academia's distaste for the "real world" as it is of dog-eat-dog, hyper-competitive parameters that necessitate total commitment from those who pursue professordom, lest they be cast out as hopelessly irrelevant.[1] Thus, academia's reputation as an Ivory Tower of knowledge, discussion, and insight that never makes it past the ivied walls of the university—where ideas might be of practical use—is perhaps not so unfairly gained.

Undoubtedly, my eventual intolerance of what I detected as the academy's nearly willful blind spots is informed by my blue-collar roots. Although both of my parents went to college, I instinctually understood from a young age that education would be my ticket out of replicating the challenging financial circumstances that my family faced, and a chance to jettison myself into a world bigger than a town where cows outnumber people six to one. While I am proud of where I grew up—(un)objectively one of the most beautiful places I've ever laid eyes on—I also understood that a hefty scholarship was the only way I could realize my goals, given that my parents were in no position to support my education. Early on, it thus became my mission to be a top student: I took all of the most advanced classes the conglomerated high school the next town over had to offer, and excelled in my extracurricular activities.

When I was seventeen (cue Frank Sinatra reference), I headed off to the University of Chicago on that hefty scholarship (and hefty financial aid package). Wondering all summer if I should have pursued trumpet performance at a music school instead, I was skeptical of everyone and

---

1   During a professional development colloquium early on in my graduate career, one professor advised us to stay peripherally involved in academia if we couldn't nab a tenure-track job or postdoctoral research fellowship after earning our PhDs, to "show our dedication." This always stayed with me; it marked when I began to wonder if this level of competition would prove unhealthy for me later on down the road.

everything at UChicago leading up to that first day of college. My reticence was amplified due to being rejected from my first choice—Vanderbilt University, which would have been a complete disaster in retrospect[2]—and so I moped around campus for a few days, trying hard to squelch my inner excitement over the tantalizingly nerdy conversations floating about the stunning gothic architecture.

It took less than a week for my dour facade to be eclipsed by an utter enrapture with UChicago, and its radical departure from the dirt roads, fields, woods, and wildflowers of my childhood. Surrounded by intellectual peers, I was exhilarated: intense, hushed discussions of solipsism, the early writings of Karl Marx, and how Noam Chomsky relates linguistics to social theory made me feel as though, at long last, I'd come home. My professors quickly became my idols and—other than the latter-stage math PhD student who made an awkward pass at me via email,[3] and a handful of other, more savory figures—most of my instructors at UChicago were bonafide professors.[4]

I declared East Asian Languages and Civilizations as my major the beginning of third year—after trying out every

---

2   OMG, *fraternity balls*?? I would have *died*. Quite obviously, I did no actual research on what kind of school Vanderbilt is and only "liked" it because its name sounded stately and cool. Plus, since I wrote my essay about how eating poison ivy on a dare taught me to never do anything for money, it's no wonder that such an Old Boy institution rejected me.

3   The email was a single line: "Love affairs are good; try to have as many as possible."

4   Today's universities outsource up to 60% of undergraduate teaching duties to graduate students and adjunct professors, who receive pitifully low wages and zero benefits. Indeed, Noam Chomsky theorizes that this is due to the neoliberalization of the University, which now has far more administrators than actual professors. If this all sounds grossly exploitative and unfair, it's because it is.

course of study from philosophy to biology. I was, and am, intellectually promiscuous, but in those days I was contracting the equivalent of intellectual STIs. I grandly decided, for instance, after one week of core astrophysics, that I wanted to major in "the closest intellectual territory to the last frontier: SPACE"—and withdrew from the course after bombing the first midterm due to a complete lack of studying. In fact, the only reason I had settled on East Asian Languages and Civilizations was because I had studied so much Chinese that I'd accidentally completed a third of the degree requirements, and no longer had time to endlessly explore other courses of study by the time we were required to declare our majors.

During my last year of college, though, I realized that there was a hole in my life: music, truest of loves from when I first waddled up to the piano as a toddler to performing at Carnegie Hall and gigging around Vermont as a teenager. Somewhat dually tinged with a kind of masochistic inner rebellion, I had dismissed music as a comparatively weak course of study upon matriculating at a university so staunchly rigorous—and perhaps even anti-creative—that its unofficial nickname is "Where Fun Goes to Die." So after taking the plunge with Music Theory for Non-Majors earlier in the year, I enrolled in Western Music History from 1800-Present, where I would soon meet an instructor who would greatly influence the course of my life.

He was a bright-eyed-and-bushy-tailed postdoc: a former Brahms scholar interested in everything from historical keyboard improvisation to video game music. Having never been exposed to "musicology"—the theoretical and social analysis of music in historical contexts—before this seminar, my mind was soon being blown on a weekly basis. Not only was the music we discussed way beyond anything I had ever heard at the time (Varese! Stockhausen! This kinda techno-sounding guy Steve Reich!), the postdoc was both a brilliant scholar and a talented pianist. He seemed so happy, so content, like he had struck that elusive balance between musicianship and intellect.

During our last conversation at UChicago, he asked if I'd ever thought about graduate school. My heart leapt out of my chest, and I leaned in as he offered what would later become life-changing advice. "You know," he cooed in his mellifluous British accent, "if you combined your Asian studies with your passion for music, you might come up with quite an interesting dissertation topic in musicology." The words reverberated in my mind like an echo chamber: a universal sign of hearing important advice if there ever was one. When I left his tiny hovel of an office—typical for a postdoc, I would later come to realize—it felt as though my life's mission was crystallizing.

I officially wanted—needed—to get a PhD.

———

MY DISSERTATION—ORIGINALLY TITLED *Liner Notes: Aesthetics of Capitalism and Resistance in Contemporary Japanese Music*—crossed the finish line at around 350 pages, with five chapters. As perhaps the primary exercise in doctoral training, a dissertation outlines the theoretical and literary contexts of a field, identifies gaps in the existing research, presents a solution through a hypothesis/argument, and hashes it out for a couple hundred pages before wrapping it all up in the conclusion. In academic writing, "hashing it out" means engaging with the work of existing scholars, considering as many points of view as is viable, and justifying why your theoretical framework is important, and superior. Then, after submitting the dissertation—which takes most people one fitful to three agonizing years to write—you prepare for the defense: a two-plus hour long session where the team of professors you've worked with throughout graduate school grills you page for page, while you field their questions on the spot. It is perhaps the most nerve-wracking hoop of all, but once you pass, you officially become . . . a *doctor.*

PhD: three letters no one can ever take away from you.

One thing no one ever tells you is that the process of writing a dissertation is really, *really* lonely, and pushes many students to their absolute limits. In my cohort alone, we developed mysterious rashes, hives, repetitive stress disorders, acne, significant and inexplicable weight loss/gain, addiction, participation in abusive relationships, insomnia, panic attacks, as well as, good ol' fashioned anxiety and depression. One of my colleagues aptly described the process as "drifting off into the infinite." Since undertaking a PhD involves conducting research no one has ever done before and literally becoming an expert in that field, it's an intimidating prospect. What's more, your committee—that aforementioned team of advising professors you assemble usually at the end of your second year in the program—continually probe your ideas from all angles to "make them stronger" (while, in actuality, driving you crazy). In the beginning, the prospect of writing a dissertation is like gazing upward at a mountain of Himalayan proportion. Weighed down by the constant stream of critiques from my committee AND the general pressure to conduct my research as thoroughly as possible, I often found myself thinking:

How am I ever going to finish—or even START this?

I wrote my diss over the course of two miserable academic years, and essentially produced two mirror documents presented as a whole. One half is your standard academic content: theoretical engagements with ethnomusicological research, and primary source analyses of capitalism and aesthetics. The second is a collection of ethnographic vignettes: first-hand accounts of being in the field that ultimately informed my theoretical perspectives, while shaping my ever-evolving personal relationship to Japanese society. In fact, my so-called "fieldwork" was basically me just living life in Japan. Separating "Jillian, the Researcher" from *Jiru,* my Japanese self, was never something I was interested in either personally or professionally.

I started writing the vignettes during my eighteen-month-long pothead phase, when I smoked copious amounts of weed to numb what was, in retrospect, the stress of writing a dissertation, feeling split between the US and Japan, and my growing dissatisfaction with academia. At the time, writing the more traditionally academic chapters seemed not only theoretically premature, but so profoundly un-fun that merely thinking of the task induced nausea. To beat the crippling writer's block and assuage my growing anxiety about not making enough progress on my diss, I began writing down some of my stories.

I sobered up before heading off to Japan on a writing fellowship for the latter half of that year. I was originally waitlisted, but was soon awarded this support after one of the professors in the department of Asian Studies came into Hai Hong, the restaurant in Cornell's adjacent Collegetown neighborhood where I waitressed on the side during my last few years in school. Having recently endured the first of what would be a series of increasingly desperate mental breakdowns,[5] I was delighted by the news. It meant I could resume my life Japan: the only place I had ever lived not as a student in my entire life, and maybe the only place in the world (other than my childhood home of Vermont) where my heart feels like it can rest. And so I set off to Osaka to write—while, of course, generally enjoying my blissful life across the Pacific.

I was so happy . . . and then I returned to Ithaca for the final push.

—

GETTING YOUR ACCEPTANCE LETTER INTO A PhD program is like unwrapping the Golden Ticket for Willy Wonka's chocolate factory.

The postdoc, it turns out, got a tenure track job at Cornell while I was living in Japan post-graduation, teaching English at two rural middle schools. I had found out when I asked him to write a letter of recommendation on my behalf for grad school applications, and he not only happily obliged, but suggested I apply to Cornell as well. The thought of working with him delighted me, and after looking up other professors in the Departments of Music and Asian Studies, I

---

5   It was intense. Having had a writing fellowship that year exempting me from teaching—and thus admonishing me from most of my human contact—I began to wade into the dreary depths of isolation that come with finishing a dissertation. Yet unaccustomed to this despair, I sent an email to my advisor expressing that I wouldn't actually kill myself, but that I could understand where Taylan was coming from. Half an hour later, two police officers showed up at the coffee shop where I was working, followed by my advisor himself. I was mortified and furious at the time, but still recognized it as a cue to take a few weeks off and visit the relaxing sanctuary one can only find at their mother's house.

felt like Cornell could be a good fit for my research project. I submitted my application in January.

Unlike for undergrad, where one receives one's academic fate via an emotionally deflating skinny envelope or a relief-inducing fat package, the postdoc wrote me a cryptic email in mid-February, saying he had "good news." I saw the message while sitting in the school staff room with no classes to teach, so I made up a bogus excuse to leave and immediately hopped on Skype once I got home.[6] When I heard "fully funded," "health insurance," and "impressed with your application," I cried tears of sheer joy and ran around my Japanese living room—complete with paper screens and straw floors—in a circle, shrieking and laughing. In that moment, I thought that I'd never have to worry about anything career-related ever again.

Excited though I was that my plan was progressing so smoothly, I'll admit that I wasn't particularly excited about moving to upstate New York for the duration of my 20's. But undertaking doctoral studies at an Ivy League institution provided me with a sense of security about my future that assuaged those inner protests. After all, in pursuing my dream of professordom, I was no fool: taking yourself out of the "normal" job market and chasing after Quixotic windmills by studying something no one ever has before you is risky business. Although I wrongly assumed that getting into a PhD program was the biggest hurdle to clear on the way to professordom, I rightly figured that there was no sense spending seven-plus years doing this unless you're playing to win. So while I was a

---

6   "I have to go to the post office . . . like, right now. *Shitsureishimasu*—'excuse me for leaving early'!"

bit apprehensive about what I had signed myself up for, I was also ready to roll.

My cohort might recall our first meeting with the Department Chair (head professor) and the DGS (Director of Graduate Studies) who, that year, was the brilliant, intimidating, old school AF professor who also happens to be the world's foremost scholar of Mozart. With Imposter Syndrome violently rearing its Medusa-heads inside of me, I tried to keep calm as he told us his rigorous expectations in the years to come. Explaining that five years of guaranteed funding from Cornell might not be enough to sustain us for the duration of our tenure as graduate students, the Chair looked toward me—the sole ethnomusicologist—and said that fieldwork tacks on at *least* another year. After the meeting concluded and the professors left the room, I turned to my cohort and asked:

"Does anyone feel like they just signed away five years of their life?"

There were two distinct phases of graduate school for me: before the qualifying exams, which we called the A-exam at Cornell, and after, when I began the slow and painful process of writing my dissertation. In the beginning, the whole PhD gig felt like Undergrad 2.0. Getting paid—handsomely, at that—to sit around tables and have discussions with brilliant people? Like, *really?* With the dissertation light years away, grad school was not only fun, but with virtually no outside distractions it was also pretty easy. Plus, there's the unmistakable mystique of hobnobbing in the academic world that makes you feel like a wizard, or a member of the Dead Poet's Society. The end-of-semester dinners at the professor's houses, for instance, were like being invited to Dumbledore's lair. Following the conclusion of our seminar on Haydn's London Symphonies, the world's foremost scholar of this composer prepared us a three-course meal in his garden—complete with wine from his personal cellar—and tipsily regaled us with tales from his own student days.

"Professor Webster, can you tell us *another* story about that one summer in Vienna?"

Then there was summer vacation. With no responsibilities for nearly three full months, we'd sit on an easy five-K of funding meant to supplement our "research" which, in actuality, constituted vacationing either at field sites or the locations of important archives. For the Western musicologists, this meant summers and semesters in Paris, London, and Krakow; for the ethnomusicologists, Bali, India and, of course, Japan. Indeed, it was as a graduate student that I cultivated my burgeoning double life across the Pacific, nurtured by summer research grants and six months to year-long fellowships, where I could run away and, under minimal supervision, "write my dissertation" between parties, riding my bike through the back streets of Osaka, exploring the trains in Tokyo, playing piano at a male ballerina's studio, dancing until morning in underground clubs, digging around junk shops for vinyl records and vintage Dior, working under-the-table as a cake baker at a champagne bar, playing dress up with old ladies who giggled at how funny kimonos apparently look on an American, and living life . . .

Beyond the guaranteed funding from one's graduate program, free money is basically everywhere in academia. Grant applications might take time to write and originality to conjure, but if they're successful, your bank account will suddenly have a pile of cash inside with basically no strings attached. Plus, there is a lot of creative licensure in stipulating the limits of one's research. I once got $500 from the music department to go to a rave in Japan for "fieldwork purposes." In defense of this seemingly egregious manipulation of university funds, my research centered on underground music, and this secret mountain party was at the nexus of both my professional and personal interests. That said, I strategically designed my research to be fun, like going to raves in the first place, so . . .

While the first few years of grad school were all fun and games—writing papers, teaching interesting classes to undergrads, submitting new work to conferences, and feeling important—the A exams during third year changed everything. A 72-hour closed-note exam of questions sent from your committee that you anticipate by assembling extensive annotated bibliographies and reading thousands of pages, the exams brought with them a sense of accomplishment and self-actualization as a scholar. They also heralded hyper-focused stress, isolation, perpetual over-caffeination[7], and obsessive thinking that I thought would be temporary.

——

DURING MY TIME AT CORNELL, I witnessed the postdoc from UChicago—who had since become one of my committee members—go up for tenure. Tenure-track jobs in academia are scarce: a handful of positions open up each year, and dozens of hyper-qualified PhDs vie for them in a ruthless, haphazard process of nearly masochistic hoop-jumping. In

---

7   During my second set of A exams, I drank so much espresso that it felt like I had four legs and eight sets of knees. Stuck on a question about the aesthetics of fascism, I took a long walk to get some of the caffeine out of my system and made some green tea upon returning to my apartment. Interestingly, my focus sharpened and I was able to concentrate for the first time in hours.

order to be considered for tenure today, a professor must teach undergrads and grads, publish a book with a second in the works, present at major conferences in the field, regularly publish in the major journals, and conduct new research all at the same time.

As for the postdoc, I saw this once happy man—with a beautiful tenured professor wife and twins boys at home—gradually turn into a husk. The physical transformation was beyond mere aging; he looked gray, hollow, and strained beyond his years. Setting up meetings with him was almost impossible, likely because he was stretched so thin with teaching commitments, writing his book, and advising duties. He avoided his inbox like a bad cliche. Books were stacked almost to the ceiling on all tables in his office, and he was often spotted—totally frazzled—wandering around campus in a daze, eating Snickers bars for dinner at 10:30pm.

This went on for years.

—

MY RELATIONSHIP WITH THE JAPANESE DJ I had met during my fieldwork and was feebly trying to date long-distance for two and a half years dissolved almost immediately upon the end of my fieldwork in Osaka and my return to Cornell. I was writing AND teaching at this point, and worked at a Chinese restaurant on the weekends. Piano studio lessons, though offering an important creative outlet, were an added commitment.

I learned "The Alcotts" by Charles Ives.

It was a tough semester, but I was both looking forward to the freer summertime schedule to finish up my damn diss, and dreading the closer proximity I'd be to my own thoughts. With no more students to shower with love and encouragement, and no more piano lessons to serve as artistic therapy, it was me vs. myself in a race to the finish line. I had just three months to finish writing my theoretical chapters, edit the whole document, defend, and get the hell out by August—the graduate school's deadline—when I would move to New York City to begin life anew.

My routine was simple: wake up, write all day long about stuff no one knows about, try to make it *worth* knowing about (and comprehendible), worry about all the different questions my committee was going to ask in the defense, attempt to prepare for them by considering everything from at least ten different angles, and then work at the restaurant at night.

Sleep for a few fitful hours, wake up, do it again.

Sobbing became a regular part of my routine, usually upon waking ("Another day of this!! I hate my fucking life!!"), and often several more times throughout the day. My family and friends could no longer relate to me, they later confided; my mom described me as a red-hot cast iron frying pan that would immediately evaporate droplets of water upon contact. I was *so* miserable.

Physically, I reached a point I'd never experienced before. I was the thinnest I'd ever been, at 6'1" and around 125 pounds. My clothes were hanging off of me; I was just skin and bones. And my skin . . . my poor skin. Pebbly stress acne peppered my forehead, cheeks, and chin. My hair was at once dry, stringy, and greasy, and my natural curls lost their luster. I felt so ugly, so unattractive—made all the more painful as I processed the loss of a relationship that never really existed in the first place, since the dude was a textbook narcissist.

And it was almost impossible to move on from it all, because he was heavily featured in my underground music chapter!

After pulling several consecutive all-nighters in the engineering library fueled by mania and cold coffee, I finally pushed "Send" on the pre-defense draft. On the way back to downtown Ithaca, I literally passed out in a graveyard and slept for several hours due to uncontrollable exhaustion. My friends—many of whom were similarly adrift at sea with their own dissertations—weren't around to celebrate, which didn't matter anyway because I wanted to be alone. By that point, I had more or less lost the ability to relate to other human beings.

I forced myself to take a week off before the upcoming defense, during which time, I began smoking weed again. I had so much nervous energy that I couldn't really relax: I stayed up too late, obsessively recorded music on piano, and worked more at the restaurant to make much-needed extra money. In one particular episode of delusional fantasy exacerbated by copious ganja use, I truly believed that I was channeling the spirit of Charlie Parker—one of my heroes—and made a giant collage of him while seriously considering getting the words "BIRD LIVES!" tattooed onto my head.[8]

When the big day came, I had decided to exercise the option to invite a friend, as dissertation defenses are technically public events. Before the defense, the professors make you sit outside of the room while they discuss your dissertation in private. Other than waiting backstage before the

---

8   Instead, I settled on a tiny letter X: a letter with anonymity, no history, and a conjurer of Malcolm X—itself a reminder to fight for what I believe in, and to remain cognizant of privilege.

Maple Festival Talent Show as a kid and slowly climbing up the big drop on the Raging Bull rollercoaster at Six Flags, I'd never been that nervous in my life.

When they called me into the room after an excruciating fifteen minutes, my committee chair sat me down. "Jill," he said softly and with a gentle smile on his face, "before we get started, we'd like to let you know that you've passed."

I . . . PASSED.

As it turns out, the defense flew by. I was both moved and humbled by the kind comments from my committee ("a tour de force, from start to finish" being the comment most etched in my memory–along with "what are your plans for publication?" and "your section on aesthetics could use some more work.")[9]. My friend later confided that she was stunned by the entire process: "I've never seen this side of you," she said, somewhat incredulously. "I had no idea what you guys were talking about, but you sounded like a genius boss." And let me tell you, in that moment, I felt like one. Afterward, I tried to herd everyone together for a picture, but the Japanist had, in my chair's words, "limped away." Those that remained shook hands and, just like that, we parted. Immediately after, my friend and I got super high on weed and we ate Chinese food at the restaurant where I worked.

———

IN THE END, MY EXPERIENCES IN academia didn't leave me permanently bitter or jaded (although there were some yucky moments of intimidation and bullying from a few professors). A few years out of the gate, I'm living a very happy life in New York City putting my PhD to good use—and as for my time in academia, I can rest easy because I know I gave it my best

---

9   Haha, yeaaaahhhh . . .

shot. My drive and determination made me a pretty good graduate student, and I'm sure that I could have landed a tenure-track job somewhere if I had stayed in the game. The final stretch toward submitting my dissertation once and for all, though, gave me reason to take serious pause. The pressure, isolation, and straight-up stress quite obviously proved too much for me, and to blindly push forward toward my dream of professordom—itself steeped in long-expired motivations—would have been nothing short of sadistic.

Having left the academy, this book is therefore an experiment in what I understand as public intellectualism: a practical, accessible application of the theory learned inside the confines of the Ivory Tower. To this end, *Japanthem* seeks to bridge the ideological nuance, rigor, and experimental thought-processes of academia with a more accessible—more fun!—popular, narrative writing style.[10] As a reworked version of the vignettes included in my doctoral thesis, the stories presented here illustrate the theoretical content of my dissertation by recounting the specific instances that directly influenced those very ideas.

Japanthem thus asks you to come to your own conclusions about what these twenty tales more broadly illustrate about music and (Japanese) society. So, while I do not explicitly state my hypothesis that capitalism may be conceptualized as an aesthetic—a musical parallel to a socio-governmental schema—there's a story about sitting in the audience of a J-pop show, and watching people who've never met sing together in unison. While I don't go too far into the concrete

---

10 Perhaps first illustrated by my creative use of footnotes. I seem to recall the legendary Professor David Rosen quipping that footnotes—often all that's left of aborted pages, or even chapters of content—are the best part of any book. Here's hoping . . .

details of traditional Japanese aesthetics, there are snapshots of traveling to a remote village in northern Japan to take Buddhist dance lessons. And while I don't wax on the underground world's inherent opposition to a diametrically defined mainstream culture, there are tales of meeting DJs in basement clubs who show us, first-hand, what it means to live against the system.

With this book, I not only aim to create a new platform for theoretical discussion, but also hope to demonstrate perhaps the most poignant feat of all: a real-world application of ethnomusicology. This is a field of study so obscure that it literally serves as the butt of a joke on 30 Rock. Yes, friends, the mysterious yet rigorous degree of Liz Lemon's hotdog-selling boyfriend that could land him no other job . . . was ethnomusicology.

But don't worry, Dad—it seems to be working out just fine.

On Noise

Noise: a kind of experimental music that utilizes electronics, synthesizers, and non-traditional use of musical instruments to create post-melodic, textured soundscapes. Having developed throughout the past forty years, Noise grew into a distinct musical and performative style in Japan by the early 1990s. Some musicologists trace Noise's origins back to the Music Concrete movement of the mid-twentieth century; others, including the author, conceptualize it as a creative appropriation of the sensory overload and commercial excess of late-consumerist societies, including but not limited to Japan.

—

NOISE IN TOKYO: IT'S EVERYWHERE, AND it's inescapable. The trains are already whirring when you wake up. Depending on how close your apartment is to the line, you can even hear the train station jingle from your bed[1]; depending on how thin your walls are, you might have heard your neighbor snoring all night. Since your kitchen is basically in your *genkan* shoe area and only has one burner that takes forever to make anything with, you head to the *konbini*

---

1   These little tunes played over the intercom on train platforms are known as *eki-merodi*, or *eki-mero* for short.

convenience store to pick up an *onigiri* rice ball for breakfast and maybe a cup of hot coffee most of them sell now for 100 yen.[2] The door beeps when the glass doors automatically open for you, and the staff shout *irasshaimase!!!*[3] in a saccharine voice that belies a misery that, in all likelihood, mirrors your own. When you're checking out, they narrate each purchase in that same voice: "Rice ball, 129 yen! Hot coffee, S-size, 100 yen! Here is your receipt! Thank you very much for coming to our store!" Meanwhile, you're blocking it all out because it's all just a *little* too loud, you know?

Soon you're at the station, ready to go to your job or maybe just get out of your tiny, tiny apartment where you hit your head on all the doors. The people working at the station shopping mall—a ubiquitous phenomenon in Japan's major metropolitan areas—are all shouting *"Irasshaimase!!"* at the tops of their lungs, along with the deals of the day. If you're at a big station like Shinagawa, Tokyo, Shibuya, or Shinjuku, all the train station jingles are playing at once now, each with a melody more manically happy than the next: *The Chuo Line Rapid Service will soon be arriving on Track 14! Passengers bound for Okubo, Higashi Nakano, and Kōenji, please take the Local Service line on Track 13! The Shōnan Shinjuku Line, bound for Atami, will soon be arriving on Track 2!*

After the automated announcers come on with arrivals, departures, and warnings to stand behind the yellow line, the attendants in the station pipe in with their own announcements . . . which are basically the exact same thing, except

---

2   This is one area of Americanization that I'm A-OK with. When it comes to coffee, sometimes *more* is more: the words of a latter-stage PhD student if there ever were any.

3   "Welcome, and thank you for your patronage!"

louder. *Then* the attendants working on the platform itself yell at you to line up—behind the yellow line, of course—and to be careful!

The train is coming!!

You can probably grab a seat if it's not rush hour, depending on the line, but all bets are off on the Yamanote and Chuo lines no matter the time of day. If it is rush hour, you'll probably be packed in so tight that your feet aren't touching the ground. *Do-a ga shimarimasu! Gochuui kudasai!!*[4] Oddly, the inside of the car is usually pleasantly quiet, with only that lolling train whir to keep you company, because Japanese etiquette discourages people from making sound in enclosed spaces.[5] Besides, people are too absorbed in their smart phones—occasionally books, more so in Tokyo than in other places—to want to engage with the world around them anyway.

After a few restfully quiet minutes, the announcements start up again: *Mamonaku, Ichigaya. Ichigaya desu. Migi-gawa no tobida ga hirakimasu. Gochuui kudasai.* Then the English announcement comes on, which is pronounced in an exaggerated accent to make sure that the message gets through: "The next station is IIIchiGAAAAya. Doors open on the right at IIIchiGAAAya." Or, "The next station is NaKAAAAno. Doors open on the left at NaKAAAAAAno."

Thanks for that! It really made all the difference—or reinforced difference, anyway . . .

Then you get off and it's another shopping mall, or sometimes a labyrinth of multiple shopping malls, and if you don't

---

4   "Doors closing! Please be careful!"

5   Someone PLEASE tell this to all the passengers on American public transport. That, and to not eat chili, curry, or any other stewed item inside the train or bus . . .

know exactly where your exit is you'll be trapped: spending forty-five minutes trying to find your way back to the other side of the station (I'm lookin' at you, Shinjuku). Even if it's a smaller station there's probably some guy standing right outside the gates screaming *"Irasshaimase!"* while shoving *uchiwa* paper fans or tissue packets in your face for the karaoke booth or drug store he's hocking for (I'm lookin' at you, Kōenji). Finally on the street, you get to hear the automated bird-tweet sounds that play at the crosswalk, advertisement trucks that drive around telling you to listen to so-and-so's latest J-pop release, political party trucks that drive around telling you who to vote for, little kids screaming because they're not old enough yet to learn about not disturbing the *fuinki* (social atmosphere), and more people shouting *"irasshaimase"* until you're ready to crawl back into the womb.

If you're lucky, your commute isn't disrupted by a *jinshinjikou*—"passenger injury"—which is most often a euphemism for people who commit suicide by leaping in front of approaching trains. They happen daily, sometimes multiple times, and with alarming frequency at the start of the new fiscal year in springtime. Everyone knows, but I never saw anyone act particularly phased by it unless it happens on your train line.

The evening rush starts at 4:30 and ends at around 8, so there's no way to avoid getting packed into the train cars, sometimes by a guy wielding a shield designed for this very purpose. You get off at your stop, and then it's back to the simultaneous announcements over loudspeakers, people advertising time sales, whatever—and you try to ignore it, feebly. When you do finally make it home, it's time to eat your crappy bento box you got for half-off before the supermarket closed and to zone out in front of your computer or phone, watching some stupid video to block out the train whirs you still hear from inside your house.

It's lunatic, never stopping.

—

I WENT TO TOKYO ON A whim. It'd been a while that I'd actually spent time there, not just out of necessity on my way in or out of Japan. The contract had ended at my place in Osaka, and there were friends I wanted to see there before leaving the country to finish up back at school. It made sense to make the trip up, originally just for three days, but I ended up extending it twice . . . although once was due to the fact that I (perhaps not so accidentally) missed my bus out of town.

The truth is that I hadn't wanted to go to Tokyo. I thought I hated it. Two and half years prior, I had left in a big hurry for Osaka because I felt like I was going crazy. My tiny room in a share house[6] in a slightly removed industrial part of the city felt so small with its paper-thin walls and two hoarder roommates—one of whom was home *all the time,* and the other spared no opportunity to point out mistakes in my Japanese, comment on my cooking or how big my feet are, tee-hee, or how "lucky" it must to have a schedule as *hima* (free, empty) as mine, given that I was in Tokyo on a research fellowship. The building was squalid, with broken electronics and garbage strewn everywhere and stray cats lurking between tall weeds in the overgrown "picnic area." As much as I grew to resent these living conditions—which weren't particularly convenient either, located rather far from the

---

6   Essentially a semi-permanent hostel, where residents, generally renting out rooms rather than entire apartments, are not bound by contract. Instead, tenants pay on a month-to-month basis.

nearest station and next to a busy highway—it took all I had somedays to leave the apartment.

If I went outside, I'd have to deal with the crowds, the bustle, the *noise* of Tokyo.

With no responsibilities other than the vague, abstract duty of "fieldwork," the boundary between work and personal time began to blur. My routine consisted of following a soulless media empire during the daytime and going to smoke-stinking basements in the middle of the night to see some angry dude bloop blorp on a synthesizer—or play an amplified fluorescent lightbulb (true story)—while tripping on acid for the third time that week. Naturally, I was rendered alienated from most people as a result. After all, I was an outsider, and Tokyo spared no chance to remind me of that. I was just another anonymous *gaijin* foreigner no matter where I went, battling off unwanted English menus at restaurants, listening to people talk about my "exotic" appearance right in front of me under the assumption that I'd have no idea what they were saying, or feebly explaining to station attendants that I understand Japanese and don't need help—that I am simply looking at the map. My world became my thoughts, and I could barely sleep; I felt as though I was sleepwalking through my days. Eventually I began to wonder: *Do I even exist?*

During a two-week trip to Osaka in the latter half of my fieldwork—similarly decided on a whim—I instantly felt more relaxed. Perhaps because it's closer to where I first lived in Japan, Osaka is just easier for me to handle than the mind-boggling metropolis of Tokyo. The cost of living is much more reasonable, and the trains aren't nearly as crowded; you don't even need them anyway, because you can bike the diameter of the city in an hour. The dialect is friendly and informal; people are much more relaxed. Everywhere you go, there's just more space. And there are trees outside—there are parks! People make eye contact with you . . . people *smile* . . .

Afterward, I based myself in Osaka without looking back. I was able to build a life there in a way I couldn't while living in Tokyo, not least because the underground music scene—my people, my home in Japan—was so welcoming. I didn't have to prove myself; I liked them, they liked me, and that was enough. This isn't to say that people *weren't* welcoming in Tokyo, but rather that Osaka is just less busy, and less self-conscious. While some of the friendships I made in Tokyo have proved to be the real deal with time, it was easy to feel lost amongst all that hustling. The Tokyo underground scene, in some ways, had begun to feel like middle school all over again: you might have a connection with someone, but if you're not able to provide social clout that'll make your new friend seem relevant to the social-climbing "party-people," well, then, *ja ne.*[7]

After laying down roots and establishing some *ibasho* (a place where one can always go and feel welcome, at home) in Osaka during my most recent long-term stay in Japan, many of my long-standing beefs with the country at large began to go away. OK, there's no way around it: I'm going to keep having the conversation about where I'm from and how tall I am a million more times, so I might as well have fun with it. Someone goes off on how Japanese food is, factually speaking, the best cuisine on the planet and that American food is terrible? Muster up some empathy to see where they're coming

---

7   See ya.

from, and maybe gently explain that "American" food comprises cuisine from our diverse populace and isn't just corn dogs and ketchup. Fruits and vegetables are inordinately expensive? Oh well, buy them anyway and really enjoy them. My apartment is minuscule and I hit my head constantly and am afraid to make any sounds because the walls are made out of papier-mâché? Go to a party to stomp and dance and stretch . . . get all that tension out with friends! Someone who's never met me before comments on how "big" I am and thinks it's funny? Make space for the uncomfortable feelings, while not taking that shit personally.

After all, in a society where being small and dainty is so highly prized, it just isn't OK to call someone—especially a woman—"big."

As this glass-half-full way of seeing things came to replace what were once sore spots, and as my relationship with Japan continued to evolve, I increasingly wondered if I could patch things up with Tokyo after our ugly break-up. After all, it was in Tokyo that I became absolutely enraptured by Japan to begin with: truly love at first sight, like a homecoming, as though I had been searching for this place my entire life without realizing it until I got there. Sure, things got bad, but how could something that felt so true be wrong? Was it possible that I had been too harsh, or had misinterpreted what was really going on? With no expectations and the help of two and a half years of distance, I went to Shin-Osaka station and hopped on the first available *shink* (foreigner slang for the *shinkansen* bullet train) bound for Tokyo.

Yes, it was still noisy. But when I found myself with some friends at one of my old haunts, listening to some dude scream and throw himself on the ground while lighting an electric piano on fire—and, later, three guys hunched over analog synthesizers sampling a robotic voice that whispered "block your inbox"[8]—something clicked. I *missed* this crazy music. Although there is a Noise scene in Osaka, I suddenly realized that there just isn't enough noise *itself* for this kind of music to make sense to me the way it does in Tokyo. In Osaka, Noise feels conceptual, like feigned cosmopolitanism.[9] It just doesn't match the city's happy-go-lucky, *nandeyanen!* (popular slang for a very loose translation of "whatever!/what the heck!/that's wack!") atmosphere, where people wear bedazzled sweatsuits out and about and old ladies brag about the crazy-cheap bargains they scored at the local *shōtengai* mom-and-pop shopping arcade.

Perhaps that's why the underground scene in Osaka is so much lighter: lounges where anyone is welcome, no questions asked—even if you're in and out of jail due to a drug addiction, even if you're a suit five days a week and only rap on the weekends, even if you earn money whipping businessmen at an S&M bar, and even if you're a foreign graduate student. Just starting out? No problem. You can practice DJing here, and you know what, let's grab a drink so you can tell me about that dissertation you're writing. Hey, who went out and bought the snacks for everyone to share? That was really nice. Let's do a special night of karaoke, where *everybody* gets to sing. House music with positive messages of love and acceptance, albums produced and released entirely by friends, neo-disco, Japanese *shitipoppusu* synth pop from the 70's and 80's, or

---

8   I *feel* that!

9   This being said, some of Noise's pioneering artists were based in Osaka and nearby Kyoto in the early 1990s, notably Hijōkaidan.

religious chants mixed with Louis Armstrong[10] . . . this is the vibe in Osaka, at least to me.

. . . Whereas in Tokyo, I once saw a guy slam his face into a cymbal, break a piece of Plexiglas over his head, and throw himself on the ground as he was playing distorted Metallica records at maximum volume, all while taunting a bunch of sweaty dudes (plus me) in a basement:

"This is too gentle for you, isn't it?"

But there I was, laughing, nearly euphoric, and totally feeling these guys playing what was, in actuality, some pretty dark music. And I wasn't the only one having a grand ol' time; it was a packed party, an anniversary show that a friend has been putting together for a few years now. For a person who covers her ears when an ambulance goes by in the US, I wondered how I could actually *enjoy* the abrasive Noise gig in a grimy little basement somewhere in western Tokyo. It was so loud that my ears felt like they were growing a coating of fuzzy cotton from the inside out: a feeling I savored as I unexpectedly waxed nostalgic about temporary hearing loss.

Ah, the Tokyo days . . . they were actually pretty fun, weren't they?

The music was dope, raw, and cutting-edge—as was the animated video someone had put together playing on the projection screen that showed jackhammers relentlessly pounding at a cyborg's head. All of it was, literally, shockingly relatable: this aesthetic somehow made sense, scratched an itch, and quenched a thirst. As I took the train home later that night—sweaty, hair matted to my forehead, and stinking of second-hand smoke—I finally got that the miserable existential crisis I had endured in the Concrete Jungle a few years prior is what allowed me to connect with Noise in the first

10 Only you, DJ Hayato.

place. I understood that the effort of trying to stay sane in the Mad City is the due one must pay to go underground. At last, it made sense that recklessly stomping and bopping in that little basement—with my people, at my *ibasho*—is how I overcame the frustration, anxiety, alienation, and straight-up rage that build up from hacking my way through the most populous metropolitan area on the planet.

I also understood that, without Noise, I'd be crushed: just another anonymous worker ant in a suit, quietly holding on for dear life, with no way out except for jumping in front of the train.

So, is the revelation at the Noise gig how I made peace with Tokyo? Sure—that, and not taking Japan Railways trains on this trip unless absolutely necessary.[11] Seriously, it's *allll* about the Tokyo Metro: chic, on-time, quiet, no infuriatingly "happy happy" train station jingles . . . and far fewer passenger injuries.

---

11 Also, a dimebag of weed.

Hate/Love

Hate

LOOK, WE ALL KNOW AT THIS point that I fell hopelessly in love with Japan, and at first sight, too—but I'm here to say that I often wish this weren't the case. After all, you can't choose who or what you love, but I'm remembering now that you can choose what to do with those feelings. The truth is that I've had a love/hate relationship with Japan since the beginning, when I was treated either like an alien queen or like pond scum, or a helpless puppy dog, or a doll . . . but rarely as anything in between (like, say, a human).

Yes, this is intended to read as a rant, with all exaggerated, scathing, and the totally outrageous generalizations that come with the territory included (truly, this is not objective by any means). Why include it? Because it's real, and no love is perfect. Plus, this voice—these feelings—come from the deep wounds of discrimination and marginalization that won't be silenced, precisely because they're ugly. They deserve to be acknowledged all the same. I've spent years and years of my life working diligently to bridge cultural gaps and "see the bright side," but life as a foreigner (in Japan) can feel extremely daunting when the microaggressions pile up. It's important for me to put it out there that some aspects of everyday Japanese socio-culture are, frankly, discriminatory—even if this might read as somewhat controversial. It's not how I feel most of the time, but it is how I feel some of the time, OK?

Japan is extremely frustrating. Everything is *perfect*—the transportation, the food, the efficiency, people's clothes, the cars, the streets, the gift shops, the parks, and the traditions—there's no denying that. But it's also TOTALLY FAKE and it drives me NUTS. I've seen people drink openly by themselves, at 10 o'clock in the morning, on the train . . . it doesn't matter. If everything is so perfect, why are so many people drinking to escape?

What's more, it seems that most people are not capable of or interested in relationships based on honest communication and commitment, and are instead endlessly fascinated by the prospect of self-sabotaging, masochistic, elicit affairs with absurdly inappropriate people. Because in Japan, once something becomes a "responsibility"—and I know this is not the image we Americans have built of them—then they compulsively start to resent it, dread it, and not-so-secretly try to avoid it . . . even if they used to love it more than anything else.

But don't get divorced if there are children involved. That would set a bad example!

With your friends, too, you never know when someone might just jump off the face of the planet. Japan invented "ghosting" long before people lived on their devices, so disappearing on a friend hits new levels of insanity in Japanese society. I mean, you might get ghosted after

someone else initiates contact—sometimes multiple times—
or even arranges the plans. Let's not forget the classic,
"*kaze wo hiita*, I have a cold, sorry," which in Japanese *really*
means "I think you're a fucking creep, and don't send me
any more messages because I want absolutely nothing to
do with you." "*Kaze wo hiita*" is literally the lamest excuse
in the book; it might even be worse than being ghosted,
because not saying anything at all at least acknowledges
that you can pick up on more subtle cues. Outright
rejecting someone with an excuse everyone knows is a lie
is extremely direct by Japanese standards, which means
that the person must think you're a full-on psychopath out
to stalk them.

"Oh, but they were just being nice and didn't want to
hurt your feelings." *Nice?* If someone doesn't like somebody
else, why even bother to make plans? Like, I didn't even
contact you—*you* messaged *me*. And now you cancelled
because "Japanese people are shy?" Oh, come on. What
does "shy" even mean here? To me, disappearing off the
radar entirely is a brazen disregard for someone else's feelings—or a pretty creative way of getting someone to feel
shitty about a lunch date they probably didn't even want to
go on in the first place. It's straight-up gaslighting—sheer
crazy-making.

Yeah, that's harsh. And I don't even totally believe it, but it
feels good to say.

But for real, I really am sick of Japanese people saying that
their society is so polite all the time. People openly gawking
at me telling me about how "big" I am five thousand times is
. . . it's just next level. It's just so *profoundly rude*. And the
worst part is, if I say something about it, it's then turned back

onto me.[1] "Oh, you took it the wrong way!" Then I've suddenly just played into some stereotype about Americans *sigh* simply never being able to understand the "subtleties of Japanese culture."

Like Fukushima. That was such a telling moment to be in Japan. My coworkers apparently couldn't have cared less about what I was going through, 10,000 miles away from ALL OF MY FAMILY AND FRIENDS. Even if they did "in their hearts" but "didn't want to make me feel embarrassed by directly acknowledging my feelings," not a single person I worked with reached out to me to ask if I was OK. Instead, they actually MADE FUN OF ME in an attempt to "lighten the atmosphere" in the staffroom. Asking me if I knew there had been an earthquake and tsunami in a joking, pedantic tone—and in front of everyone? I mean, are you *fucking* serious? To knowingly attack my intelligence and dignity in a moment of weakness is just such a low blow. To take away someone's humanity like that, and in such a vulnerable position—22 years old, a foreigner far from home as nuclear plants exploded by the minute and aftershocks rippled throughout the country, including where we were located . . .

I dunno, maybe this is all some sort of post-colonial karma, like a grand cosmic play. I will not discount the

---

1 In the fall of 2017, when I worked at a bar in Osaka, a confrontation (by Japanese standards—which literally wouldn't register on the American social spectrum) with a customer came up when this tall doctor claimed that I didn't know my own height. "I'm 186 centimeters, and I'm shorter than you! You *can't* just be 184 centimeters tall." Um . . . I know my own height, hoss, and I specifically looked it up AND double-checked a) because we don't use this measuring system in my home society and b) because I get asked this all the time in this country, constantly, every day, sometimes multiple times. I may not look like it, and in your society it may be OK to "mansplain," but I am literally a professional researcher, so go check your sources. Shit. Maybe you need to recheck *your* height.

wartime years and the tragedies that Japan suffered at the hands of America. That shit is real, and extends to the treatment of Japanese people living in the United States as well. But it's not like Japan wasn't also some evil empire, sadistically destroying the lives and dignity of millions, without ever formally apologizing to the former colonies in Asia.[2] So every time some Japanese person asks if I'm astounded by how polite Japanese people are, I have bitten my tongue.

Not anymore, man. I'm DONE.

Looking back, I held my shit together during Fukushima like a CHAMP. Despite getting inundated with hysterical messages from well-meaning-but-stress-inducing friends and family every day demanding that I "come home," I never seriously considered leaving because I cared about my students—and my greater responsibilities as an educator that I actually took (and take) seriously. And I was barely even in a position of authority as the lowly "Assistant Language Teacher" (ALT), who was treated by the majority of my coworkers like a clown—an English-speaking monkey.

"Class, repeat after me!"

Yet despite these hardships, the fuzzy feelings had me glossing over the issues between Japan and me. For the longest time, I was looking at things through rose-colored glasses. By the end of my initial two-year tenure in Japan, I even felt that this country and I had forged a beautiful relationship. Sure, there were some rough times, but some of the happiest times of my life were there, too: hidden beaches, abandoned buildings, climbing on tsunami breakers, long

---

2 The famous Yasukuni Shrine in Tokyo, notably visited by Japan's Prime Ministers throughout even recent decades, refers to the Rape of Nanking of 1937-8—wherein at least 300,000 Chinese were brutally murdered by the Japanese imperial army—as a "confused incident."

bike rides, rolling in the snow, staying out all night dancing, and bullet trains (or local trains) to the mountains or the sea or temples or ancient villages. But now, I am finally allowing myself to feel the injustices that have built up over the years; I've hit a breaking point. Something is telling me to take some distance from Japan . . . to find out if the love was real. My research project is done, my student days are at an end . . . is this not a perfect chance for a fresh start?

'Cuz, you know, when is *Japan* going to finally get hip to the fact that I tried really, really hard to find happiness there? To bring people together—even people who wouldn't have anything to do with each other if it weren't for me, like a 72-year-old piano teacher and unemployed DJs screwing around on synthesizers all day? But more than all this, it's just time for Japan to acknowledge that other cultures have their own different, BUT VALID way of doing things. A good way to start would be to notice that every culture— not just Japan's—is "unique." That's a bullshit word, too: "unique." By its very definition—resembling nothing else— *EVERYTHING* IS UNIQUE. Now I don't identify as a flag toting, gun slinging, burger eatin', cowboy boot stompin' 'Murkin, but I'm proud to be from a place that at least acknowledges cultural differences—even if, as a society, we suck at it.

Japan, on the other hand? One of their immigration policies, which requires all foreigners to write their names in Japanese script upon adopting the Japanese nationality, is uncomfortably similar to the war-time assimilation policy enacted in colonial Korea and Taiwan wherein all "subjects of the Great Japanese emperor" were forced to change their surnames to Japanese names with no relationship whatsoever to their own.[3] Perhaps, this very brand of historical xenophobia is what made me feel so rarely acknowledged as a whole, complete person during my time in Japan. Once, a coworker was astonished to hear me speak English fluently to an American friend on the phone; he was shocked that I could, apparently, speak *any* language with total mastery. Seriously people, I'm not just some moronic cretin who doesn't know how to function in the world—I just come from a place that's NOT JAPAN.

My GOD, do you have any idea how much lighter it feels to let this shit go?

Over the years, I have given so much to Japan, asked so many questions, humbled myself time and time again to learn about pretty much anything Japanese: the geography (I know all forty-seven prefectures and their capital cities, and have travelled to the majority of them—even ones like Gunma, Shimane, and all of Tōhoku), the food (I had to learn how to make some things just to survive when I first moved there after college), the music (traditional, popular, AND underground), the language (both in classrooms and in an immersion setting, the culture (religion, art, social relations, holidays, traditions), and the people (teachers, business people, free-lancers, middle schoolers, young children, old ladies, old men, hostesses, DJs, professional dancers, drunks, addicts, junkies, masseuses, electricians, and a couple of dominatrixes) . . . but now I feel that it's no longer serving me to be a "student" of Japan.

---

3 By the way, Japan's wartime assimilation policies happened to be the subject of my honors thesis at the University of Chicago, entitled: *In Search of Place: Colonial Korean and Taiwanese Identity Formation during Kominka's National Language Movement and Military Volunteer Programs, 1937–1945. And yes, I am aware that this title is terrible . . .*

Basically, Japan broke my heart.

But maybe . . . MAYBE our *en* is real. And if it is, it will unfold in a way so beautiful I can't even imagine. And the signs are all there . . . after all, it was truly *hitomebore*: love at first sight.

Love

WHEN I FIRST SET FOOT IN Japan, it wasn't even in my plans. It was an overnight layover on my way back to school in Chicago after a summer in China, studying abroad with the famously, masochistically difficult total-immersion Princeton in Beijing program in advanced Chinese. It was a poignant time for me—I'd saved up every penny I had to be able to participate, and to finally see Asia: a place I've been dreaming about for as long as I can remember, maybe because it seemed as far away as you can go (culturally *and* geographically) from my home-town in northern Vermont. Beyond sheer interest, I always felt a familiarity with Asia: I was strangely drawn to Japan as early as the third grade,[4] when I struggled to make origami birds and boxes and wrote about it for a school newsletter.[5] Later in middle school, it struck me as odd (and sad) when a classmate from the comparatively cosmopolitan, nearby Quebec brought sushi for lunch and the kids of the Irish Catholic gangs who ran the town laughed and pointed at him.[6]

. . . but what's so weird about raw fish?

The same was true when I ate seaweed for the first time in Girl Scouts . . .

. . . what a great idea it is to eat this stuff!

I even signed out the pocket Japanese language guide in the library (along with books on the abominable snowman, ESP, UFOs, and poems by the greats Shel Silverstein and T. S. Elliot) and tried to teach myself some phrases.

---

4   Actually earlier, when I asked my father at around age three: "If people from Japan are called Japanese, then what are people from China called?"

5   "It was difficult, but fun!"

6   To Marc Antoin Dunn: I'm sorry I watched those assholes make fun of you. It's really brave (and cool) that you brought sushi to Fairfield Center School—in the 1990s, no less.

"*Konnichiwa!* YA o GEN-ki de-SU ka?"

Anyway, it was an intense summer for which I had been groomed for two years. I had apparently taken to the Chinese language with natural ease, and my professors at the University of Chicago had asked to push me harder than the other students to realize what they saw as my potential to speak at the native level. I agreed because they made China seem like the best club in the world, and that the only thing you had to do to join was speak beautiful Chinese. Easy, right?[7]

The thing is, the China of my dreams—a place I fantasized about as a kid going to the one Chinese restaurant in the county with my mother as I gazed up at the fluorescent Great Wall poster, a place of ancient and mystical wisdom, temples, a society of knowing elegance—was shattered upon my arrival in Beijing. After all, it was the summer of 2007, a year before the highly anticipated Beijing Olympics, and the city was in the midst of a drastic transition: it was dusty, highly polluted, and crowded with people who looked to be dead or close to it wandering the train stations and tourist sites. Truly, Beijing was (and is) a post-Soviet[8] (/communist) jungle that seemed to have paved over the China promised by the professors back at school.

Of course, I was wrong—and in several capacities. Really, the issue wasn't China but rather my Orientalist gaze that

---

7 The thing is, Chinese really isn't that difficult because you don't have to conjugate verbs. The initial learning curve is steep, but studies have shown that people with perfect pitch (which I have) are able to learn Chinese with ease, and that around 40% of the population in China has perfect pitch themselves. This leads us to ponder an interesting "chicken and egg" scenario between perfect pitch and tonal languages, eh?

8 The city, while never formally colonized by Soviet forces, has Soviet metropolitan infrastructure, notably ring roads.

created unrealistic expectations. The amount of trauma and upheaval that China has endured is nearly beyond comprehension, and considering the circumstances, Chinese society has exhibited unfathomable fortitude, perseverance, and optimism in the face of it all. Indeed, it was this very aspect of China that not only moved me with time, but also got me to see the wisdom—the knowing elegance of the China in my dreams—that is still there . . . even if the Great Wall *is* a ridiculous tourist trap.[9]

Plus, I learned that China is still very much a society of scholars, like in the olden days when they occupied the very top rung of society (which ironically contributed to its susceptibility to 19th and 20th century imperialism). Walking past the statue of Confucius on Beijing Normal University's campus to the first of my daily *five* hours of intensive instruction at 7:20 every morning, I found myself increasingly humbled and awe-struck as the summer drew on. The teachers were STRICT, and they pushed me harder than even the professors at school. They each seemed to have overcome incredible personal challenges to be in their position—teaching at a prestigious university in their nation's capital—and they expected nothing less than sheer excellence from us students in return. Since they knew their stuff forward, backward, and surely in other dimensions, I respected them from the bottom of my heart.

Although it was a tough summer academically, sleeping around five hours a night due to the sheer volume of work we had to complete, the bonds that were formed and the love that the teachers bestowed onto us—and, of course, learning

---

9   You can, however, go to the zì rán cháng chéng, or "Wild Great Wall," which are ruins totally free from tourism.

a crap-ton of Chinese—made it all worth it. Ah, that last night Beijing going out to Beihai Park and Wudaokou for beer gardens and karaoke, selfies and strange meat on a stick, and tears and hugs . . . it turns out that the sign in our dorm that taunted us all summer was prophetic:
现 在承受 , 以后享受 *(xiàn zaì chéng shòu, yǐ hoù xiǎng shoù)*: suffer now, enjoy later.

Respect, and a deep kind of love that feels familial. I came to (and still do) think of China as something like a sibling: at once the most fun, and at times the most annoying thing on the planet.[10] Chinese public bathrooms? Good GOD. That's some next level shit . . .

. . . literally.

Since I had dreamed of Asia my entire life, and as this was just my second time leaving the US (except for Canada, but since I grew up so close to Quebec we didn't count our frequent trips up there as "going abroad"), I set off on a solo sojourn throughout inland and southern China for about ten days after the program ended to see the rest of the country. Armed with nothing but British Lonely Planet's *Pocket Guide to China* that I got for five bucks at Barnes and Noble a few days before leaving the US—and those dreams, of course—I took a series of *yìng zùo* hard seat trains from Beijing to Xi'an, Xi'an to Chengdu, and Guilin to Hangzhou. I was so excited by the unbelievable prices of these tickets— about 40 RMB, or 8 USD, to get from Beijing to Xi'An—that, honestly, even if I *hadn't* been flat broke, I would have bought them on principle because they were SO CHEAP. I thought I was one a smart shopper.

Like, how bad can it be? #hubris

---

10 That said, I annoyed my older sister far more than she ever annoyed me.

As it turns out, pretty fuckin' bad. Let me tell you, there is nothing more profoundly uncomfortable than *yìng zùo* trains ... make no mistake, this is steerage class: the absolute bare-bones way to get around China. They don't turn off the lights, there are no assigned seats and finding a place to park yourself for the next 24 HOURS OR MORE is a free-for-all with people shoving you out of the way and weaving around your legs. Everyone is crammed—and "everyone" was, in the case of *yìng zùo*, migrant workers who had apparently never seen a non-Asian person before and were therefore openly gawking at me for literal minutes at a time, touching my hair, or even stroking me.

Now don't get me wrong: I understood where they were coming from and wasn't offended by this, and I even let them touch me since it was pretty harmless (and their curiosity was warranted). The clinchers, though, were people getting wasted on the undrinkable *baí jǐu*, Chinese white rice liquor, eating plastic bags of chicken parts—including suction-packed chicken feet—with smacking lips and food particles flying everywhere, and the constant shouting about *nothing.* This included the ladies pushing carts of ramen through the aisle where people were squatting with all their baggage, shouting at the tops of their lungs at 3am:

FĀNG BIÀN MIÀN! FĀNG BIÀN MIÀN![11]

The seats were literally made out of plywood, and with a "table" that the "booth seats" shared no bigger than a lunch tray, these train rides were (and remain) the most physically uncomfortable I've ever been. By the time we got to Hangzhou, a 26-hour journey from Guilin, I was openly crying and even chanting to myself to get through it:

---

11 INSTANT NOODLES! INSTANT NOODLES!

We're almost there. We're almost there. Two more hours. Never again. Never again . . .

Of course, the trip was a life-changing journey wherein all my limits were tested: physical, financial, and spiritual. In retrospect, the fact that I made it out in one piece with literally no planning, whatsoever, is basically a miracle. I got hustled, I got hit by a van *in my face* and knocked onto the street, I got violently ill unwittingly eating spoiled horse meat, I didn't know how to pack light and was schlepping around two giant suitcases and a heavy backpack, the dialects in inland and southern China were different than the Mandarin I had studied, my friends and family basically had no idea where I was, and I had practically no money, no phone, no internet, and barely any juice on my computer (*and* no electric converter) . . .

Ah, to be nineteen years old again . . .

By the time I got to Shanghai, I felt like I had been through the ringer . . . totally burned down to ashes, utterly exhausted. Yet, I wasn't depleted. In fact, it was a curious state of peace: almost bliss. The journey was done, the mission was complete. That final morning in Shanghai before boarding a flight with the always delightful ANA airlines (*'All Nippon'* Airlines? What's *'Nippon?'*), I leisurely strolled around, satisfied with life, and thought to myself: *the only thing left to do is go to Japan for a night.*

I'll admit, a part of me wanted to stay in the airport and sleep; I heard Japan was really expensive, my clothes were all filthy, I was drained from almost two weeks hacking my way through inland China, and I wasn't sure what to do with my heavy backpack filled with Chinese textbooks and souvenirs. But when we landed at Narita International Airport—pristine and immaculate, almost eerily so—something told me to hit the town—to explore. I was excited; after all, this was Japan! It's safe, and the transportation is reliable so I'd definitely make my flight back . . . so, yeah, sure, why not? I waltzed through customs (after all these trips back and forth, it has never taken me more than fifteen minutes to pass through immigration at Narita), asked two American brosephs in suits where a good place to "grab a beer and hit the town" was, and—armed with the impenetrable force field of having no expectations whatsoever—headed out to the place they recommended:

Roppongi.[12]

I got on the train—in retrospect, it was probably the *Keikyuu* line—and was instantly amazed, perhaps because of the contrast with China. Everything here was so clean, so orderly . . . so *quiet!* Velour seats on the trains? This was downright luxury! Plus, the only other person in the car was some guy in a business suit who wasn't even staring at me. I even thought to myself, *Wow, this can't be possible . . . do I not register as hopelessly different here?*

This was my first lesson about Japanese people: that being totally ignored is actually a sign that your presence is *extremely* acknowledged. I mean, he had to notice me, right? He was ignoring me *hard*—the whole thing felt pretty ridiculous. So I stared at him as a sort of cultural chess match, but when he hopped off the train for his stop, I gave up: checkmate. Maybe in Japan, I wondered, people just aren't phased by perceived cultural differences . . .

---

12 . . . which I didn't know at the time is the seedy, yet extremely affluent neighborhood of Tokyo where the clubs for foreigners and Japanese people who want to get with them are located.

And it was right when the doors closed and the train started pulling away that I saw the man *crane his neck* to stare at me in utter amazement from his spot on the platform.

HAHA, YESSS! HUMANITY'S CHARMING, IF POLITICALLY INCORRECT, CURIOSITY KNOWS NO CULTURAL BOUNDS!

I made it to Roppongi following the subway maps easily viewable in every subway car, and as soon as I made it out onto the street, I was blown away. The lights! The crazy-curly-cute language! The fashion! The hairstyles! Driving on the left side of the street! The restaurants! The *energy*! Somehow, despite how topsy-turvy it was, it all seemed so familiar, like I'd been here before: as though I'd been searching for this place my entire life but didn't even know it. Picking a street on a whim and walking forward in a happy daze, soaking it all in, I bumped into a woman on the sidewalk.

"Hey, do you speak English?"

"Yes . . . "

"Cool! Do you wanna hang out with me tonight?"

" . . . OK!"

And this was when the night truly turned magical. We went to sushi, we went to some empty bar (it was a Tuesday night, after all) and requested Stevie Wonder to the DJ, we awkwardly danced and laughed, we went to a Don Quixote variety goods shop,[13] we gazed at Tokyo Tower, we went to convenience stores (where I was amazed by the cleanliness and the automatic doors), we drank electric

13 You'll just have to look this up if you don't know what it is. Basically, it's just *so* Japanese.

blue cocktails in an all-night café, and poured our hearts out to each other . . .

In retrospect, this was when I learned another enduring lesson about Japan and its people: that people open up to you if there's nothing to lose. We talked about everything and anything, like things we've been through, past tragedies, and all of our hopes and dreams for the future. Because we both understood we would probably never see each other again, we were able to gush to each other, fully. We could be vulnerable, because there was nothing to lose . . . and that's when I learned that maybe this Japan place and I weren't too different from each other.

After all, I'm the same way.

Complete love and trust at first sight, with no expectation: it felt so right, so true. It felt like I had become aligned my destiny; I had never been so sure of anything in my life.

It felt like home.

After the sun rose and the trains started back up, my companion insisted on treating an express ticket back to Narita. Still in a sort of blissful shock that this night actually happened, I realized:

I love Japan.

And I promised myself: I *will* live here.

For the entire flight back, despite having not slept for days, I stayed awake for the twelve hours from Tokyo to Chicago scribbling in a diary about how much I loved Japan.

And I officially declared East Asian Languages and Civilizations as my major, and got a job working as a research assistant for a Japanese film professor after returning to school.

And went through all those traumatic experiences taking Japanese.[14]

And wrote an honors thesis about Japan.

And got a job teaching English in rural Japanese public schools with the Japan Exchange and Teaching (JET) Program.

And moved to Awaji Island for two years . . .

And found a topic I could research for nearly a decade.

Yes, my relationship with this country seems to be determined by cosmic forces outside of my control. And I don't love Japan for its superficial charms, or anything it might do for me; I just love it for exactly what it is, no more and no less. It's not easy to make a life in Japan as a foreigner, but somehow I've done it again and again. And now I just need some time to know if it's real. Something tells me it is, but much like how Japan and I fell in love in the first place, it will be unplanned, spontaneous, natural, and completely out of my control.

Who knows . . . maybe it'll be like Amaterasu, the sensitive and beautiful sun goddess/giver of all light in Japanese creation myth who shut herself away in a cave after betrayals by the men in her life, Tsukuyomi and Susanoo. With no light in the universe, the other gods and goddesses realized that the situation simply had to be fixed; the antics had been taken too far, and a grave mistake had been made. So they

---

14 Much to the disappointment and anger of my Chinese teachers. Maybe the break I've called with Japan is some kind of karmic retribution for the fact that I totally ditched China for Japan—which I even described in my diary on the plane ride as "the man I ran away with." In my defense, it was totally unplanned—it just happened, and I have no regrets; it was ultimately a good thing. Also, learning Japanese is the worst because if you make a mistake, you're rarely just corrected and shown how to it properly, like in Chinese—it's instead taken as evidence that foreigners just *sigh* can never learn the "inherently difficult" Japanese language.

devised a lavish, absurd plot where another goddess was sent down to the entrance of the cave to perform a crazy, naked dance so wild that all the gods' laughter would surely pique Amaterasu's curiosity, ultimately luring her out of the cave. In the event that she would peek out, a mirror was placed outside the entrance so that she may be blinded by her own light and beauty, and thus restore light to the universe whether she was ready to or not.

It worked.

And it just so happens that the first place I lived and worked in Japan is the island where the cave is said to be.

Ah . . . who knows how the future may unfold. *#en*

Ugo, Akita

AKITA IS ONE OF THOSE PREFECTURES that people always forget about, like Missouri. It's way up in Tōhoku: an economically depressed, isolated part of Japan with only a few train lines connecting the prefecture with the rest of the country. Akita is serviced by a *shinkansen* from Tokyo, but it drives the speed of a local train once it gets up north, with each stop more remote than the next. For any new riders, there's a cognitive dissonance between how *shinkansen* only stop at the most significant places in the prefecture, and that these random ghost towns or empty ski areas must be those significant places in Akita. The Akita shinkansen always seems delayed—itself a rarity in Japan, where trains run on time to the second—for laughably unusual, provincial, down-to-earth reasons. The real-time transit updates in Tokyo often read: The Akita Shinkansen is delayed due to strong winds. The Akita Shinkansen is delayed due to a fallen tree. The Akita Shinkansen is delayed due to a bear in the tracks. The Akita Shinkansen is delayed due to an avalanche.

Local trains within Akita are also scarce, and so it's one of the rare places in Japan where you need a car to get around. The Ou-sen and the Hanawa-sen, the prefecture's only train lines, function primarily as commuter railways to get you started on your journey. These lines, infrastructurally central though they may be, only have one or two cars per train compared to the average twelve in Tokyo. And only at peak rush hours do they run at their maximum pace of once an hour. Overall, Akita embodies the very prototype of *suroraifu*: the pleasantly slow pace of rural living, where there's no need to rush.

Akita doesn't have a *meibutsu*—a food item, tourist attraction, character, or general "famous thing" that brings popular attention to the prefecture. It also doesn't have a famous cartoon mascot as part of the various tourism-boosting efforts of Japan Railways. Kumamoto prefecture, for example, is represented by Kumamon (roughly translatable to "Little Mr. BearBear-kins"), a cartoon bear with a Hello Kitty-esque hypnotic quality that propelled him to widespread popularity. Now that he's gone *zenkoku*—ubiquitous throughout Japan—his algorithmic cuteness is plastered on all sorts of household goods to take the edge off of everyday mundanities. Need a new toothbrush? This one's got that bear on it, why not?

To be fair, Akita actually does have two cartoon mascots, but they're oddly specific and woefully unrelatable to most people in Japan, and therefore not famous at all. There's that sort of creepy *kiritanpo* rice stick character that references some obscure food from an even more obscure festival that isn't even cute anyway. Then there's Sugi-chan ("Little Mr. Pine Tree"), who isn't visually displeasing, but is so aggressively uncreative that he accidentally represents the regional apathy toward participating in this strange competition at all. After all, isn't there some *real* work to be done?

This isn't to say that Akita doesn't have any socio-cultural register. It's home to the eponymous dog breed made famous by the tale of *Hachikou* (Prince Hachi), the dog who waited every day at Shibuya station in Tokyo to greet his master years after he suddenly passed away at work.[1] But even so, this beloved story isn't really considered a reflection of Akita. Instead, this dog's significant cultural import is thought to reflect the broader Japanese values of loyalty and humility, rather than the ethos of Akita's tough and high-minded people.

That said, visiting Akita is like catching a glimpse into a Japan of the past. Most of Akita is remote, unsettled, or wild, save for a few cities that couldn't escape the encroachment of Aeon malls,[2] pachinko parlors,[3] and greasy Chinese chain restaurants that define Japanese suburbia. Akita is where you can drive for hours and not see a single town, instead surrounded by towering evergreens thousands of years old densely sprawled atop some of Japan's tallest mountains with mystifying uniformity. It's where you can find silent ponds that have pooled in the highlands, where both the volcanic vitality of mineral hot springs and the breath-like purity of cold springs flow freely from rich, black earth. In Akita, you can easily find places where you can be totally, blissfully by yourself: where you can rest and recover from being "on" in

---

1   And if you go to Shibuya Station, you'll see a statue commemorating Prince Hachi outside the central gate, which serves as a popular meeting spot in the area. *D'aww!*

2   These are essentially Japanese Wal-Marts (although Wal-Mart itself does exist in Japan). A Japanese corporation, Aeon sprawls throughout Asia, selling cheaply made products, consolidating services in gigantic shopping supercenters, and running local small businesses to the ground.

3   Pachinko, effectively a form of legalized gambling, is a mix between pinball and slot machines.

day-to-day social interactions built on hierarchies and your role within them.

Who couldn't enjoy that, Japanese or not?

Akita's terrain and northern climate urges its residents to be rugged and down-to-earth, and indeed, it's in Akita where you'll see someone stomp onto the train in well-worn work boots and plop down splay-legged across three seats, or stroll nonchalantly into a winterscape with an open jacket (for reference, you would never, *ever* see this in Tokyo). Akitans are helpful, but not overly sweet or even polite. They reach out only when it's obviously necessary, and in that process accidentally respond to you as a fellow human being, whether or not you're Japanese. But after that, you're on your own— because who would want to be coddled all the damn time?

Like when you take the last bus into the remote town of Ugo for an *obon* festival[4] dance lesson but there's huge snowstorm, and absolutely everything in town is closed. You have no idea whether you can get a taxi half an hour back to the nearest train station, where you might catch the last train back to your digs in a few hours *if* it stops snowing. And so, you head to a tiny supermarket named "Bazaar"[5] because it's literally the only place on in town with the lights on, and you stick out because you're a foot taller than everyone else, and there's no way that there isn't some kind of mistake going on here, because . . . *why else would you be there?* That's when some guy turns the corner and asks if you're that researcher who's here to study the festival or something, which apparently has made the local gossip circuit, and

---

4   Hold out to *Interlude I* for a proper explanation.

5   My favorite bizarre (pun intended) grocery store name in Akita, though, has to be "Big Freck," often shortened to "Bifure." Um . . . what's a "freck"?

after you say yes, he tells you that the rehearsal was cancelled because of the storms, but better luck next time, and lumbers outside in the blustering storm in nothing but a t-shirt, snow pants, and work boots.

Then the cashier, who overheard everything, tells you to hold on for twenty minutes so she can close up shop and offers to drive you back to the train station. She gives you the keys to go wait in the car, without supposing for a minute that you'd steal it, and so you help her out by turning on the engine, and scraping off the windshields and doors. After all, since you're from a rural, unforgivingly cold place too, somehow this entire scenario actually makes sense—like you've entered some parallel dimension.

She meets you outside at the scraped-off, warmed-up car, grateful that you understand what seems to be trans-national northern socio-cultural protocol, and starts to drive you back to the station. But because the occasion is so unusual she stops at home to get her teenage daughter so that she can talk to a real-life American who is trying to learn more about Akita, because isn't that totally weird but, on the other hand, about damn time that this place got some international recognition? And you have such a pleasant conversation that she ends up driving you all the way back to the friend's place you're crashing at another forty-five minutes away . . . but there's no need to get all gushy about it. She reminds you, feigning nonchalance, that it's not like she had anything else to do.

Ugo is the kind of place where, the next month when you finally do make it to the rehearsal and are not just the only white person there but also the only person under fifty, two old ladies approach you and ask, straight-up: "Who are you, and, um, what are you doing here?" And maybe it's because you're also from a rough-around-the-edges place where the presence of outsiders ("flatlanders," rich people from Connecticut, city people, yuppies) is more confusing than overtly threatening that you somehow understand that this isn't an aggressive question. In fact, it's refreshingly direct in a society where directly saying *anything* is considered rude. Besides, it's also entirely reasonable to wonder why someone like you would even be there in the first place.

So you answer them, and they're moved that you're here to research something near and dear to them, even if it all seems a bit out there: "You're saying you came up *all* the way from Tokyo, today, for *this?* You must be crazy!" It also turns out that they happen to live in the same town where you're staying, and so they offer to carpool with you—which develops into monthly rides, lunches, excursions to local attractions, and meeting their husbands, whom they boss around and low-key make fun of, much to your delight.[6]

When it's finally August and time to dance in the festival, that's when they'll help you get dressed in the *yukata* summer cotton kimono they arranged for you to get custom-made the month before. They'll fuss over tying your *obi* belt so that the sash hangs down just right, and prim their own makeup like you're all getting ready for a ball. They'll help you put on the *hikosa zukin* mask after you decide that the *amigasa* straw hat is too difficult to dance in (since you can't see your feet in it, and you're so not at the level yet where you can do this without looking down), and help you tie back your hair so that the blonde curls won't poke out and ruin the illusion.

---

6 Two of the words for "wife" in Japanese are *kanai* and *okusan*, respectively translating as "in the house" and "the one behind." Acknowledgments to cultural differences aside, it was refreshing to see these beautiful dancing women own their general badassery in the intensely patriarchal society that is Japan.

They'll help you review any last-minute dance steps, while graciously meeting your family who came all the way from America to experience one of last remaining pockets of wild Japan, and gift them homemade pickles.

And the next year when you return to dance, they'll squabble over who gets to host you at their house: "Wait, she stayed at your house for a night? I want her to stay with me, too!" And then they'll start making plans for the next year, and the year after that . . . although you may just opt to stay in the same inn down by the mountains and hot springs for a third year to be blissfully alone in the beautiful wilderness, and reflect on the meaning of the festival, and the holiday it celebrates: to humbly remember family who has passed on to the other side.

But let's not get emotional about this. You needed the help, they could do it, and that's all. That's the Akita way.

Amerika the Beautiful, in Two Acts

Act I: Ame-mura, Osaka

I VENTURE TO SAY THAT MANY of us born and raised in the US hold a marked curiosity toward the idea of an Amerika Town (yes, with a 'k' as per the transliteration standards from Japanese to English). Americans are largely familiar with "towns," notably of the Chinese variety, along with Little Italys, Polish Villages, and other enclaves that dot the landscape of a nation-state built by and on the premise of immigrants. Just hop on a train in New York City and get off at a station of your whimsical choosing, and you will likely find yourself in a "town" that feels a world away.

Which all begs the question: what, exactly, is this experiment we call America? Or, perhaps more accurately, *where* is America?

In Osaka, it's off the Midōsuji subway line. Packed in a few grimy blocks tucked away from the neon lights of the Dōtonbori arcade, the glitzy shops of Midōsuji street, the crowds and sheen of Umeda and Shinsaibashi, the department stores and pachinko parlors of Namba, and the seediness of Soemon-cho lies *Amerika-mura*: Amerika Town, often shortened to Ame-*mura* (ah-may-moo-rah).

There's a distinct feel to Ame-mura that lets you know you've arrived, a certain chaos that somehow feels familiar to someone who grew up with stars and stripes, bald eagles, red, white, and blue, and Uncle Sam. For one, there's garbage on Japan's normally immaculate streets despite not really having public trash receptacles.[1] Signs reminding you to pick up your dog's poop are plastered onto the streetlamps, which are curiously shaped like twenty-foot stick-figure humans carrying light orbs. There aren't any public restrooms in the convenience stores.[2] Men holler at you from the street, commenting on your outfit or asking you to come to the club where they work.

People even jay-walk![3]

Clothing stores line the streets, notably the innumerable shops selling t-shirts with American pop stars giving the middle finger and/or smoking weed, caps for American baseball teams with stickers on the brim, gold chains and wayfarer sunglasses, basketball shoes . . . then there are the hippy clothing stores, where everything is loose, made of alpaca wool, and the (Japanese) staff all seem to have dreadlocks. Not to be left out are the shops targeted at night clubbers,

---

1   The lack of garbage cans is largely a security measure implemented after the sarin gas attacks in Tokyo's subways by the Aum cult in 1995.

2   In fact, this is the only area of Japan I've ever been to where the convenience stores don't offer public restrooms. So American! Do you know how many times I've had to pee in some alley in New York because no place would let me use their bathroom?

3   That said, traffic lights are strictly obeyed in most of Japan. It could be 3am in the countryside, pitch black and without another human (much less a car) in sight, and people would probably still wait until the little pedestrian figure changes from red to green (not white, like in America).

selling polyester bodycon dresses bedazzled in pounds[4] of sequins. Oftentimes blaring American Top 40 hits from the entrances, shops are open past normal business hours, operating as late as 10pm. All the same, there's a lot less neon than in the downtown hubs of Dōtonbori and Umeda, much like a typical street in Brooklyn.

You'll see jewelry parlors selling barbells and other piercings that constitute something of a taboo in Japan, where even having pierced earlobes is considered risqué by some standards.[5] In a way, these shops vaguely resemble the "We Buy Gold! Cash on the Spot!" pawn shops lining the streets in New York, Chicago, or other urban American areas, but without the distinct aspect of hustle. We're still in Japan here: there's a proper way to do things, and everything must have its place. That includes foreigners, white and otherwise, who, while not explicitly banned from pursuing careers other than the eventually soul-sucking dead-end of teaching English, have a hard time finding work in Japan.[6]

Basically, Amerika Town is a Japanese replica of the idea of America, which is ironically the antithesis of what America is

---

4 Decidedly not kilograms. Hey, this is Amerika Town!

5 While working in the middle schools, no female teachers wore earrings, nor did any of the students. When asked when I got my ears pierced, my reply—age 7—shocked students and coworkers alike. In the US, though, even babies get their ears pierced. I dare say that Claire's Accessories has hosted this unofficial rite-of-passage for countless girls and women in America.

6 Most English teaching gigs are actually assistantships, where native speakers work as Assistant Language Teachers (ALTs) under JTEs (Japanese Teachers of English). Because of the Japanese social hierarchy, this means that the ALT must defer to the authority of the JTE, even if the JTE makes English errors. Although there is a way to climb the system (find a way to remain sincere about paying respects, since it really is wonderful just to be in Japan, and find joy in your work) it can be frustrating to work in such a decidedly un-meritocratic system.

(purportedly) all about. Indeed, Amerika Town is a fabulously insightful portrait of Japan!

Continuing onward, you'll find the burger joints. To be fair, restaurants sell burgers all over Japan and it may be a projection to draw such a neat parallel between Ame-mura and other "towns" that boast authentic local fare—but there really do seem to be more burger specialty restaurants concentrated in Ame-mura. Most of these restaurants are Japanese chains, like Mosburger, *Bikkuri* Donkey (translatable as "Surprise Donkey"), and Freshness Burger. And while there is no McDonald's—more of a staple in Japanese suburban areas, surprisingly enough—there is a location of the rarely-seen Burger King in the shopping plaza across from one of Japan's most prominent mock Statues of Liberty, perched atop the roof of a building housing at least three hip-hop clothing stores.[7]

Ah, the sweet familiarity of local American business. Mmm, global capitalism—the taste of home!

In the heart of Ame-mura is its crown jewel: Triangle Park, a three-sided slab of concrete enclaved by two intersecting streets. Triangle Park is where the party starts (or ends, depending on the level of your pre-game). It's where people get wasted on the cheap booze readily purchased from nearby convenience stores, while chatting, hanging out, taking pictures, or riding skateboards. A popular meeting spot, Triangle Park draws an eclectic, rowdy crowd of foreigners looking to party, rebellious Japanese youth living out fantasies of counterculture, and partiers on their way to

---

7   The other prominent Statue of Liberty can be found on the man-made island/adult amusement park of Odaiba in Tokyo, although there are many more *jiyuu no megami* nestled throughout the archipelago.

clubs that blast EDM at top volume. Indeed, much of Osaka's nightlife is centered in and around Amerika Town, although some of these spaces—notably Club Lunar[8]—have been shut down due Japan's anti-dance law.[9]

After hitting the club, you can bring someone back to one of the many *rabu hoteru* (love hotels) in Ame-mura. "Love" is used loosely here, of course: with names like "Hotel Rose Lips," these sleazy establishments are where you rent a room with a giant mirror on the ceiling and a double king-sized bed by the hour.[10] Take a couple of wrong turns down some inconspicuous alleys and you'll find yourself in front of a string of *so-pu rando* (soapland): establishments that take you to the next level of seediness, where men flip through a catalog and pay for the woman of their choosing to wash them, and perform other favors.[11]

But no sex![12] Prostitution is still technically illegal in Japan, although this law seems less strictly enforced than one about dancing . . .

Overall, there's a rowdiness to Ame-mura, a care-free performativity defined by dreams of what it must be like to live without rules . . . to be "free." It's an experiment: an escape, a fantasy from the everyday. Because it's not

---

8   Notable, for the author at least, as the space where I heard underground music in Japan for the first time.

9   And yes, you read that correctly: dancing in Japan has been illegal in public Japanese spaces less than 66 square meters in size since 1948, save for a few years of respite here and there. While the law was largely ignored for most of its tenure, the past ten years have seen major crackdowns on smaller, more experimental clubs in Japan's major cities, including Tokyo and Osaka.

10   That said, they're a cheaper alternative to most business hotels and are also way more spacious. Hey, in a pinch . . .

11   Apparently, only Japanese men can patron most soaplands—not that this constitutes the primary injustice of soaplands, of course . . .

12   There's no way this isn't a bald-faced lie.

"Japanese," it's therefore seen as where people can let loose, rebel, and go crazy.

So, does Amerika Town feel really like home to a person socialized in the US of A?

Given that Ame-mura superficially glorifies aspects about America that I go to *Japan* to escape, I'd say no . . . except for the jaywalking. That's the clincher. There's just something about darting across the street if there aren't any cars coming—or if I think I can make it—that brings me right back home.

Act II: Kadena Military Base, Okinawa

THE FIRST WEEK OF MAY MARKS Golden Week, a string of national holidays when everyone in Japan goes on vacation, and my best friend Lily and I decided to go to Okinawa . . . along with everyone in Japan, it seemed. There were no rooms available in the capital city of Naha, so we stayed in Okinawa City instead, about an hour north. But since there weren't any hotels available there, either, we opted for an Airbnb that boasted to be right in the city center near the local attraction of Koza Music Town.

Wow, a music town? Sounds great!

While the accommodations weren't exactly five star— snails in the outdoor shower, plywood walls, flimsy 100 yen-shop cushions that were advertised as a "complete futon set" on the website—it was, indeed and luckily, centrally located. We arrived in the evening, and everything was dark, almost shockingly so.

This is Okinawa's second biggest city . . . where is everyone? Why are there no businesses or streetlights?

Throwing caution to the wind, we decided to venture out for dinner and drinks and found what seemed to be the only *izakaya* pub open in town for a delicious meal run by an eerily dignified older Japanese man. His formal dress and classic-style bar and restaurant seemed oddly out of place on the sketchy, unlit road lined with abandoned businesses that appeared to be the main drag in town. Nonetheless, in good spirits after indulging in *goya champuru*, bitter melon casserole, and two rounds of house-made plum wine, we went for a walk to hit the town, get a feel for Okinawa City—and maybe even check out Koza Music Town!

Strolling back in the direction toward the Airbnb, we noticed another big street that we somehow hadn't noticed on the way to dinner.

Whoa, how did we miss this big drag?

At first we couldn't see where we were, as there were no lights or cars, but soon we both stopped, in dumb-struck awe and horror, when we finally caught a glimpse through the hazy light of a rogue working streetlamp:

A broad street, much wider than typical Japanese blacktop. Strip clubs. Seedy bars. All-night tattoo parlors. Pawn shops. Flickering lights, but no staff—and no customers. Each building more burnt out than the next. A stark, post-apocalyptic, bombed-out feel somewhere between post-alien invasion L.A. in the movie *Independence Day* and a Cormack McCarthy novel.

It was a ghost town; we were uncannily alone.

What is this terrible place?

A janked-out Honda with no muffler and a special, non-Japanese license plate marked with a "Y" symbol suddenly careens onto the strip; two American men holler at us through the window.

"HEYYY WHERE YOU GOIN'!!!"

The car disappears through a gate at the end of the road. Welcome to Kadena Military Base: the largest American Military Base in Okinawa, and one of the largest in all of Japan.

Horrified, fascinated, we took it all in, laughing uneasily at the names of these places as a kind of coping mechanism: Bar Playaz, Amazonian Strip Club, Last Chance Saloon, Boobies Tattoo Parlor.

A dark, hurried figure approaches us on a bicycle, riding quickly away from the direction of the gate. We freeze. He stops when he sees us and, revealing his status as an ally, offers the following advice (in English) through gasps of breath: *"Don't go into any of these places."*

Don't worry, we won't.

Dumbfounded, we realized: Is this the America that the rest of the world knows, that only we "Americans" don't?

And for the rest of our time in Okinawa, as we drove past more and more bases and the protesters perpetually outside of them, we came face-to-face with the denial that we realized we had long used to protect ourselves against the intense feelings of shame, anger, despair, and hopelessness that rise to the surface when confronting the United States' international alter ego: Amerika. This time with a "k" because it's alien yet uncannily familiar, harsh and twisted. This ain't what we've been taught in the land of the free, home of the brave.

Seriously. Doesn't history tell us that America *saved* Japan from militaristic fascism?

Worth noting is that the majority of the most horrific crimes in Okinawa are committed by American military personnel.[13]

---

13 Notably rape and murder, although statistics against foreign-committed crimes are disproportionately represented in the Japanese media.

And that there are American military bases in over 70 countries on this planet.

Yes, Amerika the beautiful . . . from sea to shining sea.

Oh, and it turns out Koza Music Town is a defunct musical instrument shop in an abandoned shopping complex, next to a strip club.

3/11

For Mom and Brooke, who came to visit anyway, and for Dad, who showed how much he cares.

It was graduation, a Friday. Beloved students I had seen grow up were now moving on. My students, but also my teachers, the ones who ended up teaching me all the Japanese I knew at the time, who showed me that humanity knows no cultural bounds—until socialization firmly settles in, anyway. Writing notes, telling secrets, secretly laughing together, and confirming that, no, it's not just me, sometimes things get crazy around here. The lifelines who helped me fall hopelessly in love with Japan. We took pictures, and shed *setsunai*[1] tears.

Sometime just before three, after most of the students had gone home while the remaining teachers were finalizing last-minute details for the *enkai* banquet/drunken festival of debauchery to celebrate the end of another school year that evening, someone happened to turn on the TV in the staff room.

Flames, something about an earthquake up in Tōhoku.

But earthquakes happen all time in Japan.

For those of us not enculturated to accept this awesome force of nature from birth, there is nothing quite like an

---

1 Bittersweet, the feeling of savoring life's inevitabilities.

earthquake: the weightlessness, that initial rush of something close to excitement, how small you feel, the admission of mortality, and the humility that comes about when the earth beneath you begins to rock back and forth, bounce up and down. It was difficult to even recognize earthquakes when I first moved to Japan. Truly, minor earthquakes really do happen all the time, and while it shocked me in the beginning, I quickly learned from my Japanese comrades that they're not that big of a deal.

I supposed, for the first few earthquakes I experienced in Japan, that a large truck or something passing was shaking my entire apartment building. Upon further inspection, there was never any traffic. Then I would further rationalize that maybe I was just imagining things . . .

. . . until the swaying curtains or some other hung object gave it away.

Ohhh . . . that was an earthquake??

It's an eerie feeling, but also an important reminder that we are all merely human, sharing this earth together—well, that, and Japan is a crazy smattering of islands born of volcanoes, fault lines, and other mystically powerful life forces straight out of a comic book and its B-movie adaptation.

Anyway, there'd been minor quakes up in Tōhoku all that week, and news tends to be sensationalized. I, along with the other teachers who left school around the same time as me, didn't think much of it, and so we headed out. It was graduation, after all, and everyone was in good spirits.

"See you tonight!"

"Take care!"

"Otsukaresama desu!"[2]

---

2   "Thanks for all the hard work you put in today!"

By the time I got home a few minutes later, I got some texts from Lily, who was teaching English up in Gunma prefecture, south of the epicenter:

> OH MY GOD, there was a giant earthquake and the entire school was shaking and we were all hiding under our desks!! This is insane!! I've never experienced anything like this in my entire life! This is so terrifying!
>
> *Oh . . . is this like . . . a real earthquake?*
>
> *Yes, I'm fine, we're not too close to the epicenter. Yeah, students are fine, school is ok. But oh my god . . . there's going to be a giant tsunami. Are you OK down on the island?*

I slowly put the phone down, and gathered my thoughts.

A natural disaster?

I picked up the phone, and dialed another dear friend living closer to the epicenter to see if she was OK. No answer, no dial tone. All cell service is blocked up, no calls can get through.

I tried again, just in case—no go.

She's OK. It's all OK. You're going to be OK.

Then, a siren I've never heard before began to wail with an eerie Doppler Effect. A van with loudspeakers attached to its roof was driving around town, announcing in Japanese:

"This is a tsunami warning. Seek higher ground immediately."

Although the town where I lived was far from the epicenter itself, it is situated at the very bottom of an island where the Setō Inland Sea meets the open Pacific, and is thus very susceptible to tsunamis, destructive typhoons, and other sea-related disasters. The wave was anticipated at no more than a meter high, meaning that it wasn't particularly dangerous for us on the island. I hopped in my car to reach a point on higher ground where I might be able to see it come to shore. Afraid though I was, I was also deeply curious.

We don't have tsunamis where I'm from.

My phone rings. It's school. The party tonight is cancelled. It would be inappropriate to celebrate.

Waiting to see the tsunami roll in with literal morbid fascination, my phone rings again, this time from an unlisted number—an international call.

It was Mom.

"Honey, are you OK? I woke up in the night and just had an inkling to turn on the television, and saw something about a huge earthquake. Where are you? Are you OK?"[3]

I think so?

After watching the sea for a while, totally blank but attempting to collect my thoughts and feelings, I drove to the middle of the island away from any place with a tsunami warning to meet up with some of my other foreign teacher friends. We were all equally unsure of what exactly was happening, what we were feeling, how we should be feeling, and what came next. We had no idea what would unfold.

How would you respond to the uncertainty of this magnitude of natural disaster, especially when you've never experienced anything like it before in your life?

We got takeout from McDonald's.

* * *

— *WHERE ARE YOU. Are you near the epicenter? Are you anywhere near Fukushima?*

— *Was there any damage where you live? Are you OK?*

---

3   Mother's Intuition is REAL—especially that of my mom.

— Important message for all US citizens living in Japan: the United Kingdom and Australia have strongly encouraged foreign nationals to return to their home countries. We will continue to update you regarding evacuation mandates and procedures as necessary.

— Jill, everyone has been asking about you. It looks really bad over there. Are you OK? COME HOME.

But . . . I am home . . .

— Thank you everyone for reaching out. I'm safe. Let's keep Japan in our thoughts, and learn an important lesson about the dangers of nuclear power.

— Hi everyone, thanks for the countless messages and concern. She's safe, she went to higher ground for the tsunami and her island isn't affected. Continue to wish her and everyone in Japan well. I'll keep you updated.

— I know this message is out of the blue, but when I found out you were in Japan I had to reach out. Is everything OK? Are you safe?

I don't know.

Just remember, the info that the Japanese press is feeding you is not necessarily the truth, and when the truth comes out, it will be too late. If the US Navy is moving its fleet because of fallout, then it is time to go. Don't wait till you are not allowed to leave. This is really bad, and apparently you don't understand how bad. I'm not lying to you, just really worried. Please Honey get the hell out as soon as possible. love Dad[4]

But I can't just up and leave . . .

---

4   Email, 3/15/11. My dad is next-level funny and weird. At the time of receiving this message, though, I wanted to throw my computer out the window: " *THIS ISN'T HELPING!!*"

I find it hard to believe that the outfit that you work for in the US hasn't called all of you back. Unless you have a lead suit that you wear constantly, you are going to be exposed to severe doses of a deadly poison that has no antidote. I know how strong you are, how much you wanted to do this asian gig [sic] and how well you have done it. I am sure that every one of those kids will never forget you and the teachers will wish the next guy [sic] was as dedicated as you were. The school year has ended, wouldn't it be a good time to go. love Dad[5]

I DON'T KNOW.

* * *

SCHOOL ON MONDAY. THE KIDS SEEM slightly concerned but still *genki*[6] as ever; all the teachers, however, are freaking out. Someone leaves the TV on in the staffroom.

Oh my god . . . the nuclear plant is exploding.

The chimes ring, time for class.

I look around to see how I should be acting, to just do what the others are doing and spare them the dreadfully embarrassing task of telling the bumbling, clueless *gaijin* what to do.[7] Apparently, we're putting on happy faces to go teach the children as if the worst nuclear accident since Chernobyl isn't unfolding by the minute.

But how are we supposed to just pretend? Are we really just leaving the kids in the dark? Is this . . . kind of fucked up, or am I just being American about this?

Who are we keeping in denial?

---

5   Email, 3/16/11.

6   Full of energy, healthy, feeling fine.

7   Notably alerting us to any sort of group meeting. "Oh, we didn't want to bother you!"

* * *

THE CONVENIENCE STORES ARE ALL EMPTY. Not because people are stealing or looting or panicking or blaming or scapegoating or demonstrating or rioting or burning or yelling or crying or throwing rocks or shaming or breaking in or unleashing generations of the unfathomable heartbreak of racialized, marginalized, traumatic rage.

People are buying and sending supplies to Tōhoku, even if they don't know anyone there.

* * *

SCHOOL ON WEDNESDAY. IT'S THE LITTLE school with twenty kids, and they only need me once a week. I haven't seen my coworkers since before the disasters.

"Tacchan's family is from Fukushima. His aunts and cousins are all up there. They're OK, but no one knows where they're going to go, if they're going to stay . . . "

"Where would they even go? Are they living within in the evacuation radius?"

"The plant is still on fire, but the news says everything's ok. What makes something technically a 'meltdown'?"

"It's bad, but they're sending people in there. They're going to use sea water to cool the reactors."

"But it's a suicide mission! No one's going to volunteer for that."

"Isn't sea water a last-ditch effort? What if it doesn't work?"

The staffroom is tense. Everyone is worried, scared. It's so much to process, and things are getting worse by the day.

I am silent the whole time, just listening, observing, and running a similar inner script in my head, equally panicked but with a slightly different perspective:

What's really going on, here? According to the news everything's just fine, it's peachy and we're at work pretending everything's A-OK, business as usual. But shit is literally exploding every day, no one knows what to do, and the tsunamis are like out of a disaster movie. Are we really supposed to just wait this out?

Over in America they think it's, like, the nuclear apocalypse and that giant waves of death water are overflowing into all parts of Japan. And maybe it's sort of true, although the exotic fear factor of earthquakes gets super played up in the American media. CAN SOMEONE TELL ME WHAT'S REALLY GOING ON, HERE? Everyone in the US is trying to be nice by showing that they care, but what do they want me to do, drop my entire life and move back? I have responsibilities here, I have ties . . . I don't want to leave. Am I totally crazy?

I'm not leaving unless the US government makes me. But for real, sometimes I'm ignored so hard that it's like these people wouldn't even notice if I up and left anyway. Look at this shit . . . everyone's getting real for the first time and taking care of each other, but I'm STILL left out. Am I a human being yet to you people, or am I still just another ignorant American who could never "understand Japan" or whatever this shit is really about? What would happen if the earthquake were here? Would I be left for dead? What do I have to do to prove myself? Am I still just totally on my own here?

Why can't SOMEONE at least acknowledge my presence, my humanity!?

Welp, I got my wish—the first one, anyway.

The vice principle was troubled, deep in thought. Then she suddenly turned to me. I saw it in her eyes: that Aha! sparkle. Of course! The *gaijin*: the all-too-necessary comic relief! Just what the room needs to break this awful tension!

But she wouldn't. Not for this. It'd be too far.

In a particularly thick moment of panicked quiet that followed, a silly smile spreads across her face as she shouts:

"Jiru, Jiru!"

Oh god no.

She shakes her hands back and forth.

"Jishin! Jishin!"[8]

This can't be happening.

Now making wave motions, she explains:

"TsuNAAAAmi! TsuNAAAAAmi!"[9]

The following moment of silence was so thick that it would swallow the entire knife whole. It was a blow so low that some of my coworkers actually cringed, even if it was on behalf of the otherwise lowly *gaijin* pond scum.

I paused, and gathered myself.

"*Wakatteimasu. Totemo kowai desu ne.* I understand. It's very frightening."

What I had WANTED to say: *Bitch, you think I don't know that??*

** *Later That Day* **

I ASK THE MATH TEACHER IF I could borrow some dice for my class. She huffs.

"Jiru. Do you know about the 100 yen shop? They sell dice. Since you've asked to use mine more than once now, it would be better if you got your own."

Do I know what the 100 yen shop is? Fuck me, are you fucking serious. I've been living here almost two fucking years and you

---

8   Earthquake.

9   As so helpfully indicated by the vice principle, this word is the same in English as it is in Japanese, but with a slightly different pronunciation.

really think I haven't figured that one out yet? Is it really that big of a deal that I've asked to borrow your dice TWO WHOLE TIMES now? Fuck you for taking this shit out on me, you don't think I'm going through this same shit? You don't think I'm scared too?

"I'm sorry for causing a nuisance. Thank you for the advice. I'll be sure to get some for the next class."

Interlude I: Context, Lyrics, and Interviews

Note: all translations from the Japanese by the author.

I. Traditional Music

CLASSIC ME, THE FIRST TIME I went to the *Nishimonai Bon Odori* wasn't in my plans. I was in Japan during the summer of 2013 for a research trip, and traveled to as many *bon odori*—or *obon* dances—as possible with the intent of selecting a traditional music field site for my primary fieldwork. With Buddhist origins that seek to honor one's ancestors, *obon* is a week-ish long holiday in Japan during the month of August when, it's said, ancestral spirits visit the Earthly plane. Sort of like the holiday season here in the West, *obon* is one of the most important holiday seasons in Japan, right up there with New Year's. People across the archipelago return to where their families are originally from to spend time with relatives (living and ethereal) and relax—and yes, train ticket prices are temporarily gouged accordingly.[1] *Obon* is celebrated, and often concluded, with *bon odori* that give the newly

---

1 Ah, neoliberalism: marching forward in endless pursuit of new market frontiers, without even spiritual exemption!

returned ancestral spirits a proper send-off back to the Other Side.

It was when I just moved to Japan that I first heard the drumming of the local *bon odori* outside my window. The music lured me into the street that night, and ultimately seduced me into a decade-plus long love affair with these fascinating festivals. From the start, I was interested in how (and why) the *bon odori* festivals—and there are hundreds—differ across Japan despite honoring the same holiday. At Tokushima's famous *Awa Odori*, for instance, the festival feels like a county fair: bandstands, announcers, street food, and raucous crowds that join in on the drum circles that inevitably coalesce on the street after the formal procession ends (and after alcohol has been flowing a while).[2] But on a trip to the northern reaches of Akita prefecture to visit my dear friend Charlotte, she took me to see the local *bon odori* near her called *Kemmanai*. I was stunned by its quiet, formal, ritualistic atmosphere that was totally unlike what I was used to seeing down in Western Japan where everyone parties in the streets, Asahi Superdry in hand.

Potato potahto, right?

Remembering *Kemmanai* during my field trip in the summer of 2013, I journeyed to Akita with the Japan Rail Pass (successfully averting the seasonal gouging, too!), and arranged to crash with Charlotte's friend who still lived in the prefecture. I had an extra day before heading up north to the festival, so this friend-of-a-friend brought

---

2 There's even a popular saying that sums up the attitude of *Awa Odori*: *Odori aho ni miru aho, onaji aho nara odaranya son son!* Translation: You look like an idiot if you dance, and you look like an idiot if you *don't* dance, so you might as well just dance.

me to another *bon odori* happening that night in a town called Ugo nearby his apartment. That festival was *Nishimonai*—and as soon as we arrived, I was stunned. It was the one.

#*en*

The *Nishimonai Bon Odori*—one of the "Big Three" *bon odori* of Japan (known as the *San Dai Bon Odori*)—is unique in feel and structure compared to the nearly twenty others I've attended. Nishimonai has two songs—*Ondo* and *Ganke* (pronounced "gan-kay"), respectively—instead of just one, which is far more commonplace. Both of these songs have their own separate dances, which men and women dance in unison; at other festivals, men and women typically dance to gender-specific steps. To invoke the spirit of the festival, dancers in *Nishimonai* wear either black masks, called *hikosa-zukin*, or *amigasa* straw hats that completely obscure their faces, just as time obscures the features of the deceased in our memories. Rather than merely throwing the Earthly plane's visiting specters a dance party in the street and calling it a day, the dancers in *Nishimonai* are thought to actually *channel* their ancestral spirits through the haunting movements and mysterious attire of the ritual. Dancing to *Ondo* and *Ganke* is thus a kind of spiritual summoning more than it is a performance.

Also unlike other *bon odori*, which put the infectious pulse of *taiko* drums as their musical centerpiece, rhythm is actually secondary in importance to melody in *Nishimonai*. Played on *fue* bamboo flutes and *shamisen* lutes, both songs' melodies weave between the steady, but spare beats of the drums, almost in mimicry of the bird calls high in Akita's mountainous wilderness. The rustic

combination of wind and percussion instruments is beautifully *wabi sabi*: the Japanese aesthetic sensibility that
embraces human and natural imperfection, and which
permeates much of Japan's traditional music and art. In
these hyper-digital, post-human times, the *wabi sabi* of a
shrill note on the *fue* or a stray beat on the *taiko* drum is
rendered especially stirring.

Nishimonai's dancers glide in a circular procession through
the main street in town—which is more like an oval, really,
with sides about a kilometer long—illuminated only by iron
urns blazing with freshly cut Akita cedar. The musicians and
singers play on the second story balcony of the Preservation
Society Hall, which is by far the nicest building in town, and
are lightly amplified through speakers attached to telephone
poles. But the music is never so loud that you can't hear the
crackling fires and the windy rustles through the nearby rice
paddies, if you listen carefully.

Nishimonai is one of the oldest—if not *the* oldest—*bon
odori* performed in Japan today. Originally a harvest
dance, records of the first festival date back to the year
1280. Although the economy of Ugo hinges upon the festival, *Nishimonai* is by far the least-known, least-attended of
the Big Three *Bon Odori* in Japan. Many of the shops in
Ugo are closed for most of the year, opening up only for
that one week in August, when people actually come
through town. Just as ancestral spirits drift about during
obon, the ghost of *Nishomonai* haunts Ugo for the rest of
the year.

A. Lyrics

1. Ondo

(ヤートーセ　　ヨーイワナセッチャ)	*Yatose yoiwana seiccha*
(キタカサッサドッコイナ)	*Kitakasassa dokkoina*[3]
時勢はどうでも	*Jissei wa doudemo*
No matter the times	
世間はなんでも	*Seikan wa nandemo*
No matter the (state of the) world	
踊りコ踊らんせ	*Odoriko odoranse*
The dancers will dance[4]	
(アーソレソレ)	*(A, sore sore ["so-ray so ray"])*
日本開闢天の岩戸も	*Nihon kaibyaku ten no iwato mo*
And even [at] the opening of Japan from its heavenly cliffs	
踊りで夜が明けた	*Odoride yoru ga aketa*
The night is brightened by dancing	
(キタサッサ　　キタサッサ　　ドッコイナ)	*(Kitakasassa kitakasassa dokkoina)*

Then: improvised lyrics about the train station, the traffic, sake, and beautiful women in the audience to further establish a festive atmosphere

---

3   Wherever an English translation isn't provided—like here—this indicates *kakegoe*: shouts, calls, and sounds without meaning that create atmosphere in Japanese traditional music.

4   Indeed, *Nishimonai* has only been cancelled twice in its nearly 2000-year history: in 1945, and in 2020. Although there weren't spectators, *Nishimonai* was back in action in 2021.

2. Ganke:

(ヤートーセ　ヨーイワナーセッチャ)　　*Yatose yoiwana seccha*

揃うた揃うたよ　　　　　　　　　*Sorouta soroutayo*

　　Harvested, is been harvested

踊り子揃うた　　　　　　　　　　*Odoriko sorouta*

　　The dancer harvested

稲の出穂より　　　　　　　　　　*Inari no shutsuho yori*

　　Emerging from the [edge] of the rice field

ササなお揃うた　　　　　　　　　*Sasana osorouta*

　　Bamboo grass has been harvested

(ソラ　キタカサッサ　　　　　　*Sora kitakasassa*
ノリツケハダコデシャッキトセ)　*noritsuke hadakodesha*
　　　　　　　　　　　　　　　　kkitose

B. Interviews

1. Interview with a school coordinator for the Bon Odori Kurabu *("bon odori extracurricular club") at Nishimonai Middle School, Ugo:*

It's great that there are more people coming to the festival. When I was a kid it was really just for the townspeople, but now we can share [this] heritage with anyone. But on the other hand . . . well, for instance, some dancers wear the beautiful hand-placed, vintage silk kimonos *(hanui)*, right? Those used to hold a special meaning—you either received it from someone, or you could order it from the shop in town after dancing in the festival for a number of years. The tourists who come to town [for the festival] seem to have taken an interest in them; they've become a top-seller *(yoku ureru)*. And that's great for the local economy, I suppose, but . . . there just seems to be something lost. It's become mere fashion *(tada no fashon)*. But . . . nothing can be done, I guess *(shikata ga nai)*.

2. *Email from Yano-san, founder of* Kita no Bon: *the sister preservation society for* Nishimonai, *in response to questions I had regarding my experiences regarding the dance* [5]:

I heard quite a story about a dancer from a while back:

Sometime in the night, as she was diligently absorbed *(isshoukenmei)* in the dancing, she suddenly had an experience not quite like her body was moving beyond her intent, but rather that someone (or something) else was gently moving her body. During that time, she realized: "Ohh (ああ, *aa*), my ancestors are with me in my body, and we're here dancing together . . . that my body, as one with my ancestors, transcended history altogether *(so no zokusen to rekishi wo tobikoete ittai ni natteru)*." And when she had that thought, tears of happiness courageously came from her eyes. This happened toward the end of Ganke, during the refrain.

I wonder, is this not the central question when it comes to *Nishimonai?* Like I've told you before, *Nishimonai* isn't just a festival, but rather a sacred ceremony . . . and because so many of us who have participated in this dance have had such mysterious experiences, I can't help but wonder if there really is something otherworldly about it.

---

5   Dedicated to keeping the music of *Nishimonai* alive, Yano-san performs his own arrangements of *Ondo* and *Ganke* in styles that he hopes will attract the youth of today: smooth jazz and heavy metal. Ah, kitsch: when something is amazing in ways far beyond its original intent . . .

II. Popular Music

FOR THE UNDERGROUND AND TRADITIONAL MUSIC life-worlds, finding field sites was easy: just go to performances. Research was all the more facilitated when it became apparent that both scenes had tight-knit communities that were dedicated to preserving and performing this music, against various challenges wrought by the same encroaching force: contemporary notions of mainstream culture, which either museum-ize the past or discourage experimentation with limits.

Delineating a field site for Japanese popular music, though, was surprisingly tricky. Like all pop music, J-pop is everywhere—blasting out of speakers on trucks advertising idol groups' new releases, playing in shopping malls or convenience stores, popping up in advertisements on YouTube—but it was all but impossible to actually hear live. Most pop stars only perform at big arena concerts, and those only happen a handful of times a year. Plus, good luck getting tickets! This led me to wonder: "If it's not performed live, then where does the music happen? And if people aren't coming together to make the music themselves, where is the community?

To find answers, I had to get creative. I lurked in convenience stores, where *sarariiman* office workers sheepishly leafed through celebrity magazines; I ate lunch at maid cafes and a restaurant themed after the biggest idol group in Japan; I observed target audiences. And soon, I began to wonder about the producers writing lyrics behind the scenes, and how they were attempting to connect with this swath of society.

Not least because it isn't often performed live, it became clear that the culture of popular music is based around passive consumption, not active participation. It didn't take long from there to realize that J-pop may not be as much about music as it may be about industry. To understand the J-pop world, then, I dedicated my efforts toward understanding the connections between pop culture, economy, and politics in contemporary Japan. The interviews I managed to conduct with the Ministry of Economy, Trade, and Industry were surprising, and cast new light on the bubblegum lyrics squealed by the biggest pop stars in Japan.

A. Lyrics

1. AKB48, "Koi Suru Fortune Cookie" (Fall in Love Fortune Cookie), written by Akimoto Yasushi (2014)

What's up, Japan!

Can you hear me?

Is life gettin' ya down?

No money, no job, too much bad news?

Well, there's no REASON to be down!

It's time to get UP!

We got a hot new song that's from AKB48 to make ya feel GOOD!

Calling all you depressed, broke losers out there, disillusioned with the world . . . have we got something for YOU!

This music playing in the cafeteria . . .

As I listen casually

And without realizing it,

My feet tap to the rhythm

I can't stop this new feeling!

If you watch the music video, every swath in Japanese society—fisherman, housewives, office workers, and even some gawky foreigner backpackers *gasp*!—gets in on the fun by dancing the same wacky steps that the Girls of AKB48 all perform in perfect unison throughout the song. Now, if only the lyrics were as easy to mimic as the dance moves . . . Here's my suggestion: "ONE OF US! ONE OF US! ONE OF US . . . "

Come on, come on, come on, come on baby

Tell my fortune!

"Fall in love" fortune cookie!

The future isn't so bad

Hey! Hey! Hey!

If you wanna call in good luck, you gotta show your smile

Wow, thanks AKB48 and your "Fall In Love" fortune cookie! If I listen to this song enough times and purchase all of the group's merchandise, I'm sure I'll get paid a livable wage!

Fortune cookie of my heart

Let's start making our luck better, from today

Hey! Hey! Hey! Hey! Hey! Hey!

This isn't something to throw your life away over

OOF, this doesn't sit well when considering Japan's suicide rate . . .

Soon, there will be a surprising miracle

Real talk: I don't disagree with this message. I actually do believe that hope is necessary for happiness—and that if we stay positive and keep the vibe high, we create positive lives for ourselves. But this whole thing just feels like The Secret gone wrong. The irony of a group of schoolgirl uniform-clad teenagers, performing model citizenry within a grossly hierarchical performance context that replicates the top-down (and highly misogynistic) structure of (Japanese) society, is already twisted—but targeting an audience of jaded, hopeless individuals disaffected by the same system is really too much.

That said, I still think the AKB48 girls have it worse. After all, their "payoff" is getting ogled by a bunch of dudes who should know better than to sexualize girls young enough to be their granddaughters.

B. Interviews

1. The following two paragraphs are verbatim excerpts from outlines of the Japanese government's "Cool Japan" and "Japan Brand" initiatives, which aims to promote the consumption of Japanese culture abroad, including popular culture and music. How I got my paws on these once-classified documents is beyond me, but hey, it was ethnographic gold #en:

   The government will place Cool Japan as the national strategy and strengthen these efforts through public-private sector joint efforts to effectively transmit content based on rich Japanese culture such as traditional and regional culture and 'Japan's attraction' including Japanese food and Japanese alcoholic beverages, which eventually leads to fostering of industries and incorporation of overseas demands.

   Japanese culture in recent years has been attracting the world's attention more than before. Japanese cuisine is increasingly popular and has been listed as a UNESCO Intangible Cultural Heritage, with sushi now being enjoyed worldwide. The creation of many innovative products by Steve Jobs, who studied Japanese Zen Buddhism, has helped to popularize Zen in many places in the United States. A study by Adobe Systems Inc. (Adobe State of Create Study, 2012) has named Tokyo and Japan as the world's most creative city and country, respectively. This reflects the world acclaim and sympathy regarding Japanese culture and creativity, which undoubtedly works positively for Japan today . . . Cool Japan is a national movement encouraging the Japanese people to fully exercise their voluntary creativity in the international community. The term 'creative' in this proposal not only means the production of art-work and design work, but also the creativity of anyone that helps to develop a business and new schemes, makes innovative attempts, and forms relationships that result in interaction. [Cool Japan and Japan Brand] are expected to help Japan become a country that strongly supports its creative [sic] and continues to develop businesses that can generate new values not only as a short-term, one-year policy, but also as a medium-to long-term vision of the Cool Japan policy.

2. Below is an excerpt from my field notes, recording an anonymous interview with a cabinet member of METI—the Ministry of Economy, Trade, and Industry—which I wasn't allowed to record:

> When I asked what the overall goal of the Cool Japan efforts are, the cabinet member from METI told me, rather solemnly, that "our primary goal is to make

money," along with portraying Japan's "unique quirks" as cultural capital "able to compete with America's cultural ubiquity." He added that putting Japan on the global stage was a particularly urgent objective with the upcoming 2020 Tokyo Olympics, which will be Japan's time to shine (and rake in the revenue from tourism).

How does METI plan to put Japan on the socio-cultural map more than it already is? By "introducing Japanese popular culture to the world," which will thereby increase tourism through Japan's "inherent appeal." I pointed out that the pop culture industry is a risky basket in which to put all of one's eggs due to its inherently fickle nature, citing the striking lack of popularity of K-pop in Japan just five years after the height of the Korean Wave, and the failure for the *Hallyu* movement to generate lasting international interest in Korean culture—popular or traditional—even in Japan. Taking pause, my interlocutor rather unconfidently replied that such a scenario shouldn't happen because "this is Japan, not Korea," and added that failure simply isn't an option: too much money involved at this point for any other outcome to be thoughtfully considered. Specifically, 15,500 million yen (or around 155 million US dollars) has been invested in Cool Japan initiatives.[6]

Later that evening, my interlocutor sent me the following email:

---

6 Wonder how all this is working out, now that the Olympics have been pushed back, spectators weren't allowed, and international travel has been banned since 2020 . . .

I am pleased to hear from you that the meeting with METI went well and the result was beneficial to you. I look forward to your research will materialize [sic] as a quality product and I am excited to read it. Though you might have disappointed at some part of our disarray among governmental agencies [sic], but I am hoping that you will continue to be a supporter and fan of Japan.

III. Underground Music

FROM THE START, I KNEW THAT the underground would not necessarily be defined by a specific sound, but by an attitude—a lifestyle. The music itself is, in many ways, secondary to the principles of resisting conformity, taking risks, and exercising free genuine self-expression. You might even think of the underground as existing in a Gestalt, positioned vis-a-vis a suspicious mainstream that lulls its inhabitants into what Henry David Thoreau called, "quiet desperation."

So it makes sense that, due to Japan's anti-dance law that was briefly banned in the mid 2010's but reinstated in 2018, a lot of the underground music is dance oriented. Even though the styles may range from smooth, pulsing techno to buoyant, neon-hued house music to "acid house death rave,"[7] dancing bodies in Japan inherently enact a certain amount of resistance. It also explains why some guy poking around on a synthesizer in Brooklyn isn't necessarily "underground," even if the sound is similar to his Japanese counterparts. What's really at risk for him?

---

7   As described by DE$TINYBRINK's Mad Scientist himself.

Plus, as an incubator of the Next Big Thing, underground music is always changing to stay characteristically ahead of the curve. Many of the artists I spent time with during the course of my fieldwork have waxed and waned in popularity in the years since—or evolved to keep their sound fresh. So, while the music I describe is probably hopelessly outdated five years after the bulk of my fieldwork in the underground music world was conducted—and you'd be surprised how many academic books, published a decade after research, claim to be contemporary—the underground attitude (hopefully!) remains the same.

A. Lyrics

1. Nature Danger Gang[8], "Ikiteru," excerpt (2015)

生きてるってなんだろう　　　　　*Ikiteru tte nandarou*

I wonder what it means to be alive

生きてるってに　　　　　　　　　*Ikiteru tte nani*

What does it mean to be alive?

生きてるってなんだろう　　　　　*Ikiteru tte nandarou*

I wonder what it means to be alive

生きてるってに　　　　　　　　　*Ikiteru tte nani*

What does it mean to be alive?

生きてるってなんだろう　　　　　*Ikiteru tte nandarou*

I wonder what it means to be alive

生きてるってなに　　　　　　　　*Ikiteru tte nani*

8　A group that dressed in elaborate, colorful costumes perhaps somewhat insensitively dubbed as "neo-tribal" before eventually—and inevitably—stripping naked at most of their performances.

What does it mean to be alive?

生きてるってなんだろう   *Ikiteru tte nandarou*

I wonder what it means to be alive

生きてるってなに   *Ikiteru tte nani*

B. Interviews

1. *Interview with Mitsuki-san, owner of a local record shop in Osaka, about my concept of "Social Media Economy" as the underground's negotiation with capitalism:*

   Social media is . . . yeah. Obviously it's not exactly good for social relations: it takes people out of the present moment, it's all about image, and honestly, it's pretty creepy. And it's definitely weird that people build themselves up on social media for whatever odd reason—to build a following or something, maybe. But since I run the [record] shop . . . I mean, it's inevitable: I *have* to use it to stay relevant. The same thing goes for shows [I organize]. If there isn't an online flyer, I'm worried that there'd be no way for anyone to know about it. It's unfortunate, but it is what it is, I suppose . . .

2. *Interview with a popular underground DJ about whether underground principles and ideals are fundamentally sustainable, or realistic:*

   Yeah, it would be great if I could be a DJ and work at the record store full-time. But to me, the stress of having to scrounge for a place to live and for food would take away from the energy I use to actually make my music. It's also *mazui* (literally, "[in] bad taste") to essentially rely on friends and family so that you can live life that way. It's their choice if people in the scene want to live like that, and not my responsibility to take care of them.

En, *Underground*

IT WAS ONLY AFTER I HAD been awarded a Fulbright-mtvU fellowship, that I considered adding underground music into my research. In fact, even pop music was a rather recent development in the way I was thinking about Japanese music at that time: a move inspired by the fellowship's application requirements, to be frank. This isn't to say that I wasn't interested in Japanese pop music and society before, but rather that, like any "good ethnomusicologist," I had only been considering the traditional music, dance, and general feel of the *obon* festivals to answer what remains the central questions of my research: Why is it that music is able to bring people together into communities—and what is the relationship of these communities with contemporary (Japanese) society at large?

Since I had begun thinking about this question in conjunction with space-time relationships—the music of the past and the music of the present—it suddenly occurred to me that underground music might provide a nice theoretical balance as music of the *future*. I wasn't exactly sure how the research would take shape, but it seemed like solid enough reasoning to move forward with the hypothesis. To be honest, I didn't even know what "underground" meant at that time either; I just pitched my revised idea to mtvU as "minimal techno," which they ate right up to seem hip to the young people. I knew that I'd recognize whatever this music was when I heard it.

The inspiration to explore underground music was born from experiences I had several years prior, when I was teaching English on Awaji Island in the Setō Inland sea where I lived for two years. Osaka wasn't too far once you're on the mainland, so every so often I'd go there to have rambunctious weekends that I simply couldn't have on-island. After all, Awaji didn't have any nightlife to speak of, and I didn't particularly want to be seen by my students or anyone else in the community.[1] I was teaching kids, you know?

Not that I did anything particularly wild in Osaka. Yup, getting lost on the trains and trying to find the Midōsuji Subway Line in Umeda Station . . . another craaaazy night! If I were with a friend, I'd *maybe* drink some cheap plum wine in Triangle Park and stay in the nearby capsule hotel (one of just a few in town that allow women to stay!) in Amerika Town. Much like Lindo Jong's character in *The Joy Luck Club*, who was introduced to San Francisco's Chinatown by an acquaintance and told that it was where she would learn all she needed to know about life in the Big (foreign) City, I was introduced to Amerika Town by an acquaintance who has studied abroad in Osaka and felt like I was let in on a great secret. Now you'll be hard-pressed to see me hanging around there, but at the time it was all I knew.

---

1 Seriously, I was something of a local celebrity. "Jiru, I heard you bought bananas at a supermarket far away from the one near your house. What were you doing all the way up there? And do *all* Americans eat bananas?"

My little excursions off-island began to evolve when another acquaintance, this time from my undergraduate days at the University of Chicago, moved to Osaka, and offered to show me places outside of the touristy Amerika Town/Shinsaibashi/Namba area in the city's center. He was an eccentric fellow: the kind of person who wears a skirt not for any statement on gender identity, but because "it's just more comfortable." He also once told me, so serious as to seethe with rage over such an injustice, that humans should have "at least" six arms. Given his unconventional outlook on pretty much any topic, it makes sense that he was into underground shows. I'm not sure how he found out about these clubs—online streaming sites like Soundcloud, maybe—but all that matters is that when he took me with him to my first show, I felt like I was home.

As a young foreign woman living in the countryside with a bunch of older people—the statistic for the tiny island of Nushima, where I once worked, was easy to remember: 70% of the population over age 70—I felt the acute pressures of being an outsider in Japan. My coworkers at the school didn't exactly make me feel welcome, either. ("Don't call her Jiru "*Sensei*"; she's not *really* your teacher.") But in the tiny basement at Club Lunar (rest in peace)—and, later, Compufunk records back when it was still in Kita-horie and that one place that was just some couple's apartment that they turned into a lounge at night (where was it . . . Unagidani, maybe?)—amongst the soft persistence of minimal techno-ish beats and nodding in solidarity at the other outcasts, similarly there by themselves, I felt like I could *relax*.

Like it was OK to just be myself.

So when it came time to do fieldwork on underground music, I followed my intuition: a rather underground approach, if I do say so myself. I knew that the music had probably changed since the Club Lunar days, but I also knew that the music would probably be electronic and techno-ish. Additionally, I intuited that the music would be found in small hole-in-the-wall clubs, like the ones I'd been to in Osaka, that you needed an *in* to find. This time around I'd be in Tokyo, a city with a metropolitan population of 38 million. Since I didn't have a Tokyo *in* when I moved there in 2014, I hopped on to *Resident Advisor*—an online magazine and database for electronic music shows and releases—and searched for "minimal techno shows." Sure enough, I found one that weekend at a place in Shibuya called Club Module (rest in peace) with no big-name DJs in the lineup.

Perfect!

The music was fine—a bit amateur and pedestrian (like techno Eurobeat)—but the place itself was exactly what I was looking for: tiny, dirty, and unable to accommodate a big audience (and big-name artists). After that first show, where I met some like-minded people, I decided to hang out at Module for a while to see what passed through, hoping for the sound of *right now* that I would recognize only when I heard it.

That wish was fulfilled with the group DE$TINYBRINK, who were just finishing up a set when I walked in the very next weekend. It was two guys with a lot of wires on a fold-up table: one playing a Roland-TR 707 drum machine, the other on a hybrid analog-digital modular Korg synthesizer. The guy on 707s was bobbing his head back and forth like a super cool turtle who didn't give a *shit*, while the second guy looked pretty out there, like he was living the *lifestyle*: emaciated, a partially-shaved head that he obviously did himself, and probably high. He looked like a mad scientist plugging and un-plugging color-coded cords into his synthesizer that produced different sounds of post-industrial, intergalactic grit. At the end of the set, he got so into the music that he punched the wall behind him in rhythm with the 707s.

Whoa whoa whoa, who was THAT?!

It turns out that Module was hosting a show with musicians who normally perform at another club, the cozy and chic Bar Ringtail, in nearby Harajuku. This was when I learned that scenes tend to form around place, or perhaps space. The owner of Ringtail, for instance, supports new talent, like DE$TINYBRINK, while also supporting more established figures, like Hair Stylistics (formerly known as the Noise legend Violent Onsen Geisha [*Bōryoku Onsen Geisha*], formally known as Nakahara Masaya).[2] This means that he organizes shows to highlight talent, and allows artists to practice in the space or organize shows themselves.

The Ringtail crowd seemed like a tight unit, descending upon the normally empty-ish Module en-masse. And they all seemed so different from the typical Tokyo-ite, with button-downed cardigans and designer handbags. These people were *cool*: into dope music, vintage clothing, purposefully mismatched earrings, crazy fur hats, pins and stickers, neo-spiritual jargon, clove cigarettes, sunglasses at night *inside*, conversations about being different, about capitalism . . .

---

2   In addition to being a legend in underground Japan, helping to spearhead the Noise scene back in the early 1990s, Nakahara-san is also a best-selling novelist—and a friendly, helpful person who continues to dedicate himself to smaller performances with his ever-changing sound. He also seems to enjoy using the *kawaii* stickers in Facebook Messenger . . .

Even though I had stumbled across exactly what I didn't even know I was looking for—a band that seemed totally now, and a group of people critical of capitalism—I still made efforts to go to other shows and check out different vantage points of non-mainstream Tokyo. One of the flyers I'd picked up at Module was for another "minimal techno" show at the decidedly mainstream Club Air, famously featured in the film *Lost in Translation*, and decided to check it out, just to see which way the wind blows around the Concrete Jungle.

After being swept up in a group of European travelers on their way to pre-show cocktails (hey, why not, and they treated), Club Air was where I caught my first glimpse of what I came to think of as the White DJ Phenomenon, a recreation of uncomfortable colonialist power dynamics: mediocre but famous white dudes from the US or Europe who headline the show and play on the main floor while local, less famous Japanese DJs play in the smaller "salons" (sometimes spelled as "saloons").[3] Turned off by the expensive 2500 yen entrance fee and the German DJ playing downstairs in the main floor that everyone was fawning over, I hung out in the salon, leaning against the wall, and sipping a drink while contemplating when I should take the train back home to the *shibui* (rustic, worn-in, yet oddly charming) neighborhood of Ōimachi.

But then I heard the sound of breaking glass . . . and mixed-metered break beats . . .

DJ Edamame: a musician born and raised in Tokyo who had recently returned from Germany, where he played with

---

3   Many of the more famous clubs in Tokyo, like Air, Club Asia, Soundvision, Liquid Room, Unit, and surely others have this set-up: a big dance floor for the main DJs, and smaller rooms for supporting acts.

local DJs and released an EP. His sound was urban and dark, yet playful—it creatively samples abrasive sounds tempered with a steady, danceable groove that make them sound effortlessly, if oddly beautiful. After dancing until the end of his set, wishing it had lasted longer, I introduced myself. He was friendly and accommodating, and we chatted for a bit before he invited me to a small party happening that weekend at a basement recording studio in Shinjuku.

In what turned out to be my first all-night show (hanging out until the trains start running again at around 4:40am[4]), I miraculously found the tiny space and was pleasantly surprised by the vibe. His show this time was different. Instead of DJing, he performed live on an analog/digital synthesizer with an electric keyboard attached. There were maybe four people in the audience, and the set was dope: raw, loud, but melodic and danceable. *Sasuga* ("that's just like," "that's so") Edamame.

We chatted after his set outside the soundproof doors, and he shared a bit about his background. Half Japanese and half European, he mentioned that he felt like an outcast growing up, which is probably why he ended up running in this scene; it found him more than he found it.[5] For DJ Edamame—who regularly performs with a banner on his DJ booth that reads "Fuck the System"—life in Europe was a

---

4   The fact that the trains don't run all night in Tokyo adds to the club culture. Cabs are prohibitively expensive in Japan besides, so if you miss last train, looks like you're in for quite a night.

5   Interestingly, DJ Edamame is not the only *ha-fu* (slang for half-Japanese) in the scene. The other member of DE$TINYBRINK is half Japanese-half African American, and confided that he has similarly felt like an outsider growing up in Japan. Perhaps it comes as no surprise that those who challenged mainstream normativity gravitated toward the underground music world: a space dedicated to expanding the periphery. It's also no surprise that I found myself there.

source of inspiration. He found the lifestyle so much more relaxed, with balance between work and leisure time more favorable than that in Japan. Indeed, he confided that life in Japan felt stifling, and the energy required to make a living competed with his desire to make music.

A little way into our conversation, he began asking *me* questions: How long have I lived in Japan, do I play music or DJ, who else have I been following so far in the underground for my research? Freshly excited from my encounters with DE$TINYBRINK, all of whose shows I had starting catching, and with whom I was now connected on social media,[6] I asked if he'd ever heard of them. In what remains one of the most beautifully fantastic coincidences I've ever experienced, his face lit up, and he said: "They're practically my best friends. We play together all the time."

So there we were, sitting in a basement in Tokyo with ringing ears, having found the same tiny scene through two completely different entry points . . . in a city of 38 million people.

#en

---

6   Which I had originally deleted for months before going to Japan this time around. After hanging out at Club Module, I realized that shows receive most of their publicity online in the form of digital flyers. And so, I re-joined the masses . . . although it was a glorious few months to be free of the hivemind.

The Dance Teacher

IT TOOK SOME TIME BEFORE I figured it out, but the message was still loud and clear: the head dance teacher in the Nishimonai Preservation Society didn't want me to dance in the festival . . .

. . . maybe. This is Japan. Who knows what she was *really* thinking under the *tatemae* mask?

As with many Japanese confrontations, her tactics were very subtle and could be infinitely interpreted. It takes a lot of humility and many years in Japan to learn to sacrifice ego and accept that even—or perhaps especially—the sweetest compliment could mean just the opposite. That said, the gestures of encouragement offered by the Dance Teacher also seemed to be laced with the biting assumption that I would be too ignorant to understand the real message. How do I know this for sure? I don't, and I may not ever, but I can say that our interactions always left me feeling embarrassed and sort of bad about myself.

So, with the jury still out on what she actually felt about me dancing in the festival for not one but now three years and counting, I present to the reader a collection of evidence which, despite ostensible helpfulness, shows that the Dance Teacher wanted me out of there.

Exhibit A: The Hustling

AFTER THE FIRST OF THE MONTHLY dance rehearsals held from January to August each year at the Preservation Society building in Ugo, I introduced myself to her, bowing to an appropriate depth and politely offering my business card with both hands, in Japanese fashion.

"Hello, my name is Jillian Marshall, and I'm a PhD student from Cornell University in the USA. I'm writing a dissertation on music and society in Japan, and am interested in this festival as an example of traditional music's place in contemporary society. I first saw the festival last year, and it seems very special. I will be coming to Ugo every month for rehearsals, so if it is not an inconvenience, perhaps we can chat sometime? I'd like to know about your experience dancing in the festival and teaching the steps."

Nice! I told myself. Direct, but not overly so. To-the-point, but respectful. Open Ethnographic Sesame!

Unexpectedly, she turned sour; it was only for a brief moment, but the shift was palatable. She looked like she had just swallowed a tablespoon of baking soda. After gathering her thoughts for a moment, she sweetly replied:

"Oh, if you're curious about the festival, why don't you look at the brochures in the atrium? They're 600 yen."

The brochure? That's basic! Reading the pamphlet and calling it a day isn't exactly great research methodology . . . surely she knows that. Is she insinuating that I'm not a serious researcher or something? Either way, I already picked up brochures in both English and Japanese on my research trip out here last year, and they are most certainly not 600 yen . . . they're free.

"Oh, and the first thing you should do is buy the instructional DVD so you can practice dancing between lessons every month, as you'll need it."

Okay, whatever. Hey, this thing is 40 dollars! Is she just trying to get as much money out of me as she can? What's she really saying?

In the end, I did purchase the DVD, and it actually turned out to be crucial in learning the steps. But as far as I know, she didn't insist that the other novices buy the DVD before moving forward.

Exhibit B: The Sandals

"OH, IF YOU WANT TO PRACTICE dancing seriously, you'll need the *zouri* (straw sandals). But . . . (giggle) I'm not sure if your size is available. The shop only carries up to extra-large."

. . . um . . . that wasn't necessary, but okay, whatever.

"Haha, how embarrassing for me! Extra-large should be fine."

Yet after this put-down, she escorted me through the snow to a disorganized little souvenir shop around the corner from the Preservation Society Hall. Mixed message much? There, a man who seemed much more enthusiastic about me dancing in the festival, asking questions and so forth, happily sold me a pair of extra-large sandals.

They fit just right—but I still wasn't sure if the point of what happened was to bring me one step (pun intended) closer to dancing, or to actually discourage me altogether by attempting to make me feel insecure over my giant and disgusting ogre *gaijin* feet.

Exhibit C: Missed Connections

I TRAVELLED MONTHLY FROM TOKYO TO Akita for the dance rehearsals, and asked if we could find a chance to meet with evasive responses every time: "Oh, you should talk to Yano-san from the sister Preservation Society, *Kita no Bon*. Oh, you already have? OK then." In subsequent lessons we ended up having no interaction at all except for an obligatory *eshaku* nod-bow at the start of rehearsals.

In the spirit of ethnographic detective work, I decided to ask Yano-san about the Dance Teacher in one of our email correspondences, which had begun months before she had rerouted me to him. How long has she been dancing? When did she start working with the Preservation Society? Do you think she might be willing to chat with me?

In the equally important spirit of intuiting when to just drop it, I learned from the total lack of acknowledgement of these questions in his response that, when a Japanese person doesn't want to talk about something, he or she might just act as if you had never brought it up at all. Coincidence? I think not.

Exhibit D: "Spider Legs"

The last two dance rehearsals leading up to the August *honban*[1] are held at the nearby Community Center, which boasts a larger space to accommodate the increased attendance, as well as live performances of *Ondo* and *Ganke* to get everyone excited. Many of the attendees for these later rehearsals are from distant cities of Sendai or even Tokyo; they learn the dances remotely as part of a

---

1   The festival itself.

larger hobby of dancing in *bon odori* around the archipelago. But because they don't come to the monthly rehearsals, they're something of outsiders: apart from the community, and dancing with a mechanical rigidity rather than with spiritual focus.

It was an interesting moment: the bumbling *gaijin* was more of an insider than some of the Japanese people.

That said, by the rehearsal in June I had experienced a series of revelations regarding these dances. The movements are simple and slow, but require intense concentration to execute properly. The best dancers look as though they're floating on clouds, moving effortlessly. While I hadn't yet achieved that level of fluency, I had become increasingly aware of my physicality, the rhythm, and the importance of quieting my mind while dancing. Really, this dance was redefining my relationship to my body, as well as to the idea of dance itself. And since I had been attending every rehearsal since the winter, the locals—who treated me like a bona-fide Akitan once these strange people from Sendai started coming—noticed my progress, particularly two veteran dancers that adopted me as their *kouhai* junior protégé back in February. I thought of them as my Fairy Godmothers.

After the June rehearsal, the Fairy Godmothers rushed up to share rare words of praise:

"That was really beautiful. Once you make sure that you keep your hands at eye level on *Ondo*, it'll be almost good to go!"

"You didn't miss a single step in *Ganke!*"

Some locals chimed in, too:

"You've really made progress! You're doing it better than we are!"

"Wow, you look Japanese!!"[2]

Feeling a bit more confident, and seeking as much feedback as possible in preparation for the festival, I decided to approach the Dance Teacher to ask what she thought.

"Well, it's looking OK, but you take giant steps like *this* (stomps legs). They have to be delicate and smooth. But because you're so *big* and have legs that look like a spider's (giggle), it looks a bit . . . strange (giggle)."

. . .

Okie dokie then.

Arg!! Is anyone telling me the truth?

Exhibit E: The Yukata

DURING THIS SAME INTERACTION, I ASKED her about protocol in the *honban*. I had heard that you need permission to dance—was that true? And if so, might I be able to dance? What should I wear? Do I have to buy the gorgeous, but extremely expensive kimono made of hand-placed, vintage silk from kimonos used in the festival hundreds of years ago that the veteran dancers wear, or can I wear a *yukata* cotton summer kimono that I've seen others don the night of the festival?

"Oh, you can dance in the *honban*, but you would want to wear a silk kimono. Sometimes we can loan them out if we know the person, but since you're so *tall* you'd have to get one custom made. That would probably cost . . . oh, on the cheaper side, around 300,000 yen.[3] And they take six months to make."

---

2   Possibly the highest compliment from a Japanese person.

3   Around $3000.

Excited that I was apparently allowed to dance in the *honban*, but devastated that I couldn't afford to get the kimono and that it wouldn't have been made in time anyway, I asked my Fairy Godmothers what to do. Slightly taken aback by the misinformation I was given, they defensively informed me that you most certainly *can* wear a *yukata*, and that, while I'd still probably have to get it custom made, they could get me a deal where it would only cost 30,000 yen.[4] And I could wear it for years.

So the next month, they took me to a kimono shop where one of them used to work and graciously hooked me up with a beautiful purple *yukata*, complete with the red lining required for it to be deemed festival-ready. We then played dress-up for a few hours, putting different silk kimono on me just to see what they'd look like while cooing, taking pictures, and laughing at me—playfully, anyway.

Exhibit F: The Classroom Observation

IN MY CORRESPONDENCE WITH YANO-SAN, as well as talking with a friend who worked as an ALT at Nishimonai Junior High School in Ugo for four years, I learned that the Preservation Society runs a temporary *bukatsu* club activity specifically for teaching interested students the *Nishimonai* dance or music, called the *bon odori* club. Although most kids in the area know the basic steps simply through osmosis I was curious to see how this tradition, which the Preservation Society believes is an important facet of local identity, is passed on to children. I was also curious to see if the pedagogical approach in the club would be different from the rehearsals.

---

4   Around $300.

So, I emailed the school and arranged to meet with the vice principle, as well as observe a class of the *bon odori* club. I took a series of *shinkansen* up—this time from Kyoto, where I was crashing with DJ friends—totaling over eight hours of one-way travel. I walked to the school after taking a bus to the center of town, and felt waves of nostalgia wash over me as I walked into the school. The shoe boxes! The chimes! The calligraphy hung in the *genkan* entranceway! Working as an ALT down on Awaji Island six years prior, I would have never imagined that I'd someday be slipping my feet into the brown guest slippers and being spoken to in *son-keigo*—the most polite form of Japanese—by the vice principal of a middle school, escorted to the meeting room, and given iced coffee by the tea lady.

Indeed, when I worked at the junior high school, the tea lady wouldn't even wash my cup because I'm a woman and should "do it myself." Which I did, and wouldn't have minded doing if it weren't that I was the only woman that she told that to.

Sigh.

Anyway, it turned out that the vice principal had some business to attend to, so I chatted with the assistant teacher of the *bon odori* club who worked under the teachers from the Preservation Society, who volunteered their time to instruct the children on how to play the drums, flutes, and shamisen, and of course, dance the steps. After learning that interested kids from the entire region join the club, that the community considers teaching the dance in school one of the most important steps they can take in ensuring the festival's continued relevance, and that she is personally worried that the increase in tourism is taking away from

Nishimonai's sacred atmosphere, she took me upstairs to observe the class.

Of course. I should have known. How could it not have been? It was none other than the Dance Teacher who volunteered from the Preservation Society to teach in the *bon odori* club.

When the teacher I chatted with introduced me to the class as I bowed and cringed, internally willing for the attention to be appropriately shifted away from the *gaijin* and back to the children, the Dance Teacher and I made brief eye contact. To this day I can't be too sure, but I detected something close to a—gasp—smile! Much like a shooting star streaking brilliantly through the night sky, it was gone nearly as soon as it appeared. She quickly averted her gaze, as if coming to her senses, and busied herself with concern for the kids.

At some point in the class when the kids were busy practicing the steps, I approached the Dance Teacher, bowed, and said an appropriate nicety. Other than giggling nervously, she didn't say anything. And for the rest of the class, she ignored me so effectively it was as though I wasn't there at all.

But in that golden moment where she smiled and made direct eye-contact with me, I sensed a curious mixture of surprise, and something faintly resembling respect. That she perhaps was beginning to see that it takes tremendous effort to make a sixteen-hour round-trip journey to observe an hour-long rehearsal; that it takes a foolhardy dedication to get in contact with everyone who I think could know about the festival and its meaning in the community, especially when there have been blocks; that, by the graces of friends in the area and my Fairy Godmothers, I could find out about this class in the first place.

That my very un-Japaneseness is paradoxically the only way that I could humbly, if intensively, pursue learning about this festival.

Exhibit G: The Honban

MY FAIRY GODMOTHERS CAME TO THE *ryokan*[5], complete with *tatami* straw mats and *shoji* paper screens, down by the mountains, to meet us. They looked gorgeous in their kimonos—they wear the beautiful silk versions—and full make-up. Their hair was tucked away with intricate braids so as to not poke out from under their hats. I, as per their instruction, hadn't started getting dressed, not least because I didn't—and to this day—still don't know how to put on a *yukata*. Does the left side go over the right, or is it the other way? One of the styles is only worn at funerals, and I don't want to offend anyone by doing it the wrong way, so, they helped me with everything—including my curly foreign hair. My mother and stepfather, who had come from the US to see the festival, remarked that it was like watching four women get ready for some kind of ball.

After around half an hour of tucking, tugging, squeezing, pulling, and pinning, they had suited me up and we were ready to go. The night of dancing was finally upon us.

And I was nervous!

Arriving in Ugo by car twenty minutes later, we parked at the Community Center, hydrated, and headed out to the main street in town, where the dancing takes place alongside woven steel urns ablaze with fresh Akita cedar. The singers, drummers, shamisen lute players and bamboo flutists—

---

5   A Japanese-style inn.

dressed in standard festival gear of *yukata* and *tenugui* towels wrapped around their heads to catch the sweat—play from the balcony of the Preservation Society building right in the center of town. Thousands of people lined the streets in bleachers, standing or sitting on tarps in the otherwise ghost town of Ugo.

Two years ago, I came here for the first time and gazed in awe at this beautiful, mysterious, deceptively difficult dance; a year ago I promised myself I'd learn it. And here I am tonight . . .

The first hour or so of the festival is when the local children, who learn the steps in school in the *bon odori* club or from their relatives, get the chance to perform and set the overall atmosphere for the festival. This is when people eat the street foods like smelt-on-a-stick, drink and chat on tarps, find their assigned spots in the ticket-only bleacher seats, browse the kiosks selling knick-knacks ranging from towels to lanterns emblazoned with graphics of iconic poses in the dance, or sample local sake. After a short break, the drums beat a rhythm signaling the beginning of the second, serious dance, where the veterans and others who (in theory) practiced hard perform. This procession is the one that all of the people descending upon Ugo these three nights in August have come to see.

I was to dance between them so that I could follow the moves from behind, and could be taken care of in case of an emergency (shoe pops off, mask comes undone, *yukata* drags, what have you) from behind.

Here we go!

As we entered the procession, I coached myself:

You've got this! You've worked hard, and you deserve to be here, even though you're not Japanese or whatever. It's going to go well. Let's make the most of this experience!

Interestingly, a few Japanese male dancers were exiting the procession at the same time. They were clearly from out of town: their movements were exaggerated, unfocused, and obviously under-practiced, and their sloppy *yukata* weren't the standard colors of the festival. The big give-away that they were out-of-towners, though, was that they were raging drunk.

Stumbling through the steps, they shouted at each other and gaudily interacted with the audience with attention-seeking poses and gestures, completely disregarding the fundamentally spiritual element of the festival that one can only learn by spending time in Ugo and actually talking to people there. It was embarrassing to watch, and I knew that if I behaved even remotely similarly, I'd probably be personally escorted out of the procession and banned from dancing in future festivals for all time. But because they were Japanese, we all just turned the other cheek without mention.

Had she seen this, I wonder what the Dance Teacher would have thought.

* * *

ONDO IS PERFORMED ON LOOP FOR the first half hour or so. It took a few rotations before my self-consciousness began to wane, but soon I found myself in a kind of trance-state. The song, repeated dozens of times, didn't grow stale; instead, I became deeply engaged with the rhythms and melody, uniting with it like breath. I felt increasingly connected with the procession as a whole: less like an individual and more like a link in a long chain, hundreds of dancers all moving as one.

It was also *hot.* The dance is slow enough that it takes several rotations to get past areas where there's blazing fire.

And even if *Nishimonai* is way up north in Akita, it's still August in Japan: inescapably hot, muggy, and *sweaty.*

There are a few exit points in the procession, and we took one which would lead us directly to vending machines where we could buy some much-needed water. Lifting up my mask to imbibe, there were gasps from nearby watchers.

"What?! She's a *foreigner!*"

"Foreigners can participate? Who knew?"

Even before I revealed my true identity by literally lifting the mask, I had heard similar deliberations from the audience while dancing:

"Wow, that dancer sure is tall. I wonder if she's a *gaijin?*"

"But why would a *gaijin* dance in this festival? How would she learn it?"

"I guess you're right . . . but her legs are so long. And look, her feet are so big! Haha!"

"Yes, but the dancing's not bad. It's clear that she's practiced. She *must* be Japanese."

"Strange, but I suppose you're right . . . WAIT! LOOK! Is that blonde hair coming out from under the mask??"

"*Yappari!*[6] She is a *gaijin!*"

Had she heard this, I wonder what the Dance Teacher would have thought.

Conclusions: A Counterargument

I MAY NEVER KNOW WHAT THE Dance Teacher thought of me being there, and it mostly doesn't matter. I am confident in the integrity of my actions and I made real relationships

---

6   Meaning "as expected." It can also mean just the opposite, depending on context. In this situation, however, it's safe to say that suspicions were confirmed.

with people in Akita as a result of working hard to learn the dance. Plus, it's healthier to let go of worrying about what other people think than to catastrophize worst-case scenarios. Nonetheless, even though it stung to never have won her outright approval (although that surprised smile during the classroom observation can't be discounted), I can understand where she was coming from.

Here comes this walking caricature of an American, bopping along with her blonde hair and her blue eyes and her toothy smile, and her mission. She likes Japan, and she wants to learn about this tiny pocket untouched by rampant Americanization! Tee-hee! But as a child, the Dance Teacher endured life in the Empire resisting the Western Barbarians and suffered through the Pacific War, when the Americans with their blonde hair and their blue eyes and their toothy smiles, and their mission, were dropping nuclear bombs on civilians, children, and animals. And later, she likely saw the Americans driving around in Jeeps, telling the naughty Japanese how to be a proper nation state with bubble-gum disregard for a society that has existed for thousands of years, all while foisting upon them this thing called global capitalism: the very apparatus that threatens *Nishimonai*'s existence today. Even now, it's still the Americans who come to Japan and get too drunk and too loud on vacation, commit hopeless social faux pas like walking into a house without taking off their shoes, and commit crimes on military bases that sprawl throughout the archipelago.

She has every reason to not trust me.

And how sickeningly ironic it is that it's an American conducting a research project asking the same questions about this festival that the dancers and festival organizers and local schoolteachers are asking themselves. Is it not topsy-turvy that an American has tapped into this struggle, and is just as concerned about the uniformity sprawling in the wake of globalization—Westernization—as an older generation of Japanese, who recognize less and less the country they call home? It's simply absurd that the American was more often than not the only dancer younger than middle age in the rehearsals[7], while the young people of Ugo don't show much interest in it beyond obligation, much less the dedication to come to rehearsal every month, much less from Tokyo.

How can it be that this is the world we live in?

I'm not sure either, but it is what it is. And with the humility that I have learned by spending time in Japan in the first place, I accept that.

---

7 It should be noted that other foreign twenty-somethings joined the rehearsals on one or two occasions. From chatting with them, I learned that they were mostly ALTs living in the area who wanted to connect with local culture; in one instance, an ALT brought a friend visiting from the US to give her an "authentic" Japanese experience. These examples only underscore my point.

Idols You Can Touch! (As Two Scenes)

THE FOLLOWING SCENES CATALOGUE SOME OF my field research on Japanese idol groups, specifically a girl band named AKB48, a contraction for Akihabara 48. The group was designed by producer and marketing mastermind Akimoto Yasushi. He envisioned a "democratic Idol group" that would be comprised of 48 members for each letter and number of the group's name—so, 240 members total. The girls, whose age ranges from mid-teens to their early twenties, are elected by their fans, and perform daily either through live performances at the AKB48 theater, televised variety show programming, or the occasional arena show (which, as of 2014, were selling out almost immediately). Sister groups to AKB48 exist all over Japan and even other parts of Asia, such as Jakarta's JKT48—all controlled by Akimoto Yasushi. In my original dissertation, AKB48 got an entire subchapter where I explored what I called the "aesthetics of fascism."

1. The AKB48 Variety Show

IT WAS JUST BEFORE 4:30PM AT Akihabara station. I had come out here from my room in a dingy share house in south

Shinagawa ward to join the crowds of *sarariimen* gathering outside of the AKB48 Cafe and Shop in hopes of catching a screening of the group's variety show. Strolling up to the ticket window, summoning up strength, and swallowing a fair bit of pride to willingly participate in whatever it is that binds together this pretty dejected-looking group of souls, a sign informed me that one cannot buy a ticket; instead, numbers are drawn to determine who gets to see the show. Sure enough, two schoolgirl uniform-clad staff members emerged from the café and began pulling numbers from a box emblazoned with AKB's logo.

Shot down, utterly.

I strategically returned to the theater on a damp and rainy afternoon when it seemed likely less people would be willing to wait outside for their number to get called. The hypothesis was proven correct with a comparatively scant crowd. In a stroke of *en*, my number got called: only one of twenty-five allowed in the theater. Upon entry, my bag was screened and all of my belongings were put in mandatory coat check. As I headed to my assigned seat, I quickly noticed with swelling dread every other person there is not only male, but middle-aged—easily old enough to be fathers or even grandfathers to the girls (or to me, for that matter). Then we were handed complimentary sugary drinks in big, plastic novelty cups—also emblazoned with the group's logo—along with a survey to be filled out at intermission. There were four questions, the results of which would conclude the evening's program: Who do you think will make the best wife? Who will make the worst? Who seems the most pure? Who seems the naughtiest? I asked the staff member if I can take a copy of the survey with me.

Absolutely not.

The rabid enthusiasm of the other audience members belies that most everyone there had seemingly come in anticipation of seeing what I had wrongly supposed was the disappointing 8 Team: the lowest-ranking "team" in the group. This means that these men are familiar with hundreds of these adolescent girls. Many of these men are wearing t-shirts with the pixelated faces of their favorite girl underneath their business suits, or are wielding signs, paper fans, or towels with declarations of their fandom scrawled across.

Soon the girls of the 8 Team come out, dancing and lip-synching in unison to one of their songs, and everyone in the audience except me joins in. The juxtaposition between the audience members' behavior outside and inside the theater was jarring: outside they didn't so much as look at each other, yet inside they hooted and howled as the girls slurped udon noodles and chirped precocious tongue-twisters resembling sexual innuendos. It was as though they had entered a zone where there were suddenly no rules, and they could let their *honne* (one's true thoughts and feelings) run free without the constrictions of the *tatemae* (one's mask).

When I left, I felt dirty, guilty, and generally kind of violated.

2. The AKB48 Pachinko Parlor

IN MY WALKS AROUND TOKYO TO get a sense of pop culture's presence in everyday life—and to simply get out of the roach hole I called home in the nine months I lived there—I saw my fair share of pachinko parlors: smoky, seedy, noisy, hyper-stimulating spaces where lonely *sarariimen* gamble on modified pinball machines, hoping to hit the jackpot against algorithmically determined odds. Long disgusted and yet fascinated by these places, whose machines and décor often have themes to appeal to niche markets, it seemed like research gold when I stumbled across a few AKB48-themed *pachinko* parlors.

It took almost those entire nine months to muster the strength and courage to venture into one. I even enlisted the support of two American friends who were visiting Tokyo at the time, and somehow convinced them to come in with me for an observation or maybe even a quick game: "C'mon! It's just *so* Japanese!" Immediately, the stench of cigarettes nearly overwhelmed us, and other than a cursory glance vaguely and skittishly acknowledging that people from The Outside had arrived, no one looked up from the machines. Walking through the isles to find a machine we would play, some of the other patrons squirmed uncomfortably in their chairs.

Just like the crowd hoping to see them live, no one was looking at each other or talking to one another. Uneasily, we put 1,000 yen—about ten dollars—into the machine, which featured pictures of some of the more famous members both on the machine and as the inner background. We tried to figure out the rules: Wait, *where* are the balls supposed to go? How do you know if you've won? How many balls do you get? Oh wait, the machine is blinking and playing some AKB48 songs! The girls just popped up! Oh, wait—where'd they go? What's happening now? Wait . . . is it *over*?? What a rip off!

Start to finish, we were only in there for about twenty minutes: enough time to realize that the whole experience is like entering a sensory deprivation tank. All three of us felt dizzy and disoriented when we left, as though we had just spent twenty minutes in a black hole.

The Secret Mountain Party

AFTER REALIZING THAT THE LARGER FORCES of *en* seemed to have brought us together at that basement recording studio show in Shinjuku, DJ Edamame let me in on a "secret mountain party" happening a few weeks later in the woods not far from Mount Fuji. He wouldn't be going, but DE$TINYBRINK was, and after asking if I was cool with drugs ("um . . . yeah, sure, whatever"), he suggested that I get in touch with the synthesizer player from DE$TINYBRINK so that we could go together. I was both excited and nervous—from what I'd sensed and heard, this Mad Scientist character was living life on the edge: playing around on a synthesizer in a tiny apartment for eighteen hours a day in Tokyo's western outskirts with no job other than writing album reviews for an online music magazine when he needed fast cash. And at that point, I'd only sort of talked to him once in person, when he was making his way through a crowd of people at a headphone concert[1] that DE$TINYBRINK played in an art gallery where he shouted over the crowd: "HEY, you're the researcher, get in touch sometime!"

---

1   A show where everyone in the audience receives a pair of high-quality over-the-ear headphones that the musicians' sets are then broadcast through. It's surreal: everyone moves and dances together without a sound being heard.

Initially skeptical, my gut nonetheless told me that I should pursue this. It was a once-in-a-lifetime opportunity, and my underground research was lining up more perfectly than I could have ever planned myself—not only had I found a scene, the scene itself seemed interested in adopting *me*. A few days later, the Mad Scientist actually beat me to the punches by finding me on Facebook and sent a message. Apparently, Edamame had already suggested to him that they take me along, and the Mad Scientist said I should "sneak in their van."[2] Again, I was both excited and nervous. Do I go away for a weekend to a "secret mountain party" with a couple of dudes I hardly know who seem pretty intense, or do I make the "sensible" choice and stay in Tokyo?

My father, in fact, was the one who inspired me to make what is, in retrospect, the obviously correct choice. "Hey, go with the band, be safe, and have a good time. Did I ever tell you about the first and only time I tripped on acid? One of the brothers at my fraternity slipped it to me, and I was so freaked out that I wandered around Orono (Maine) at thirty below zero with my jacket open, crying . . . but boy, I played one hell of a game of darts that night."

So on November 1st, 2014, after pulling an all-nighter celebrating Halloween in the clusterfuck that was Shibuya that night (thousands of people crammed in the street that devolved into a *nampa riotto*[3]), I wearily hopped on a series of trains to

---

2   This was all in English—since he's spent so much time abroad, the Mad Scientist spoke quite fluently, peppered with interesting slang that seemed at once jarringly out of place, but also entirely fitting of his overall punk-y vibe.

3   *Nampa riotto:* a type of riot that forms when men grope women en-masse on streets flooded with people, as in Halloween or festivals. *Nampa* basically translates as (a man) "hitting on" (a woman); interesting to note is that this situation is not referred as a *chikan* (groping) riot.

meet Mr. Drum Machine while the Mad Scientist took care of getting the gear into the van. Mr. Drum Machine and I grabbed a quick coffee at Starbucks—it looked like he had been up all night as well—where he gave me the lowdown on where we were headed. "We're, uh," he said shyly, "basically going to an illegal rave." When the Mad Scientist finally showed up—unapologetically late, of course—he was wearing sunglasses despite the rainy weather and a scarf tied around his head, looking very much the part of the eccentric artist Edamame had said he was. And then we hopped in the van and drove eight hours to Yamanashi prefecture, at which point the Mad Scientist immediately whipped out a pipe and started smoking weed with one hand, and steering with the other.

Here we go . . .

As we approached to our destination, I felt as though I had entered some new dimension where things were moving at warp-speed. I had only known DE$TINYBRINK for a little over a month, and here we were, spending a weekend together at a rave in what was turning out to be an extremely remote campground in the mountains. The road kept winding up and up, passing through one-way bridges and tunnels. The guys kept shouting *yabai, yabai!*[4] while I quietly savored the drop in temperature detectable even from inside the car, grateful for acting on my instinct to pack warm clothes. When we finally arrived, I paid the surprisingly cheap 2000 yen entry fee, received a pin and some stickers, and checked out my digs for the night.

415: a semi-annual party held in the woods, organized by a small group of friends in Tokyo and Kansai, the western region of Japan notably home to Kyoto and Osaka. It turns

---

4   "This is so crazy!"

out DE$TINYBRINK was invited by a friend of this group, and since they didn't really know anyone there, they set up camp and started grilling up some squid legs, vegetables, sausages, and other classic Japanese barbecue foods by themselves, while I ventured off to actually listen to the music by myself.

Instantly, I was struck by the vibe of the party. In no way was it like my image of a typical rave, where everyone dances together in Huxeleyan-like uniformity (complete with soma! . . . or MDMA, anyway) to cheesy EDM with that pornographically orgasmic beat-drop. Instead, it was a small-ish group of what seemed to be hippies, some of whom even had babies, dancing, chatting, eating outside, and getting warm near the bon-fire. The music was also totally unlike anything I had heard in Tokyo, but was equally dope. A group called Teahouses, based in Tokyo but in another scene than the one with which I was running, was playing a set that literally made me stop in my tracks. Three dudes on synths and one guy on a microphone uttering in a bratty voice that cut straight through my entire soul: "I had a dream. I had a dream, but it died. I had . . . I had a dream . . . I had a dream, but it died." Then nonsense syllables.

I felt like I was on the edge of the Earth.

Next came Friendly Giant: another Tokyo-based DJ who sometimes ran with the same crowd as Teahouses, but more so with a DJ named Labyrinth who, in addition to spinning pulsatingly dark yet danceable music, organizes big parties to support his friends from all over Japan (and abroad). Friendly Giant's style is immaculate, with a selection of fresh tracks with a round, soft electronic sound that are all somehow perfectly in persistent, seamless rhythm with one another. Again, I was floored: this was beyond anything I had expected. And the sound system! The group of friends who organize 415 bring all their own gear to make a wall of speakers with a sound that's at once loud, yet soft: like being surrounded by a womb of electronic sound without any sharp edges.

In fact, it was music and sound I had been searching for my entire life without even realizing it. The truth is that I've always been interested in dance music, but growing up on the dead end of a dirt road in a rural border town in northern Vermont, there couldn't have been any kind of music more out of place. Nonetheless loving anything with a fun, free, and danceable beat, I secretly listened to the copy of the copy of the Venga Boys CD burned by my mom's boy-friend's brother's daughter on a portable CD player in my room, and secretly savored whenever the DJ played the *YMCA* between Kenny Chesney and Brooks and Dunn at my middle school dances.

Oh no . . . "She Thinks My Tractor's Sexy" *again?*

In classic Friendly Giant fashion, every song was as play-fully driving as the one before it, and I was praising my lucky stars. This wasn't a fluke; it truly was exactly what I was looking for. In a way, it felt as though my entire life had lead me to this moment, which was at the intersection of both personal and professional interests. It was around this time that one of the guys who had joined the DE$TINYBRINK barbecue came to find me to make sure I was "OK" *(um, yeah man, just listening to the music we drove eight hours to hear)*, and also when I realized that maybe this Mad Scientist char-acter was a little too cool for school. Why wasn't he here listening to this dope music, playing from a twenty-foot wall of speakers assembled by friends?

They eventually did come out to see what was going on, but since they weren't going on until five or six o'clock the next morning, there was no scrambling anticipation to set up. While the Mad Scientist seemed entirely unphased, slumped over in a fold-up chair looking completely bored, I was growing increasingly curious about this eccentric-looking dude I had noticed all night, who was apparently a DJ as well. In fact, most of the people there were other per-formers, and those that weren't were friends who had come with them, like me. When I first saw him dressed in his bright red pants, a mint-green sweatshirt with tiny dinosaurs all over it, a brown fur hat, neon-colored sneakers that looked like space shoes, a giant gold chain, and oversized novelty glasses, a part of me recognized him:

I know exactly who you are. You're whimsical, you're out there, you're always smiling and cheerful, but you're actually shy, reserved, and maybe afraid to be your real self . . . you're like me.

So despite not having slept in days, I waited until around 1 am for him to start playing, at which point he stripped down to nothing but skin-tight, rainbow-colored sequin shorts in the cold mountain air while the speakers behind him bellowed his stage name:

"DIGITALBOY!!!"

Expecting to hear something darker than the mani-cured house music set he had put together, and finding the whole strip tease-thing to be a grandiose display of narcissism—and a bit over the top for where I was at that night energy-wise—DIGITALBOY's set marked when I decided to go to sleep. In what would later be untrue, I told the Mad Scientist: "I respect his sound, but it's not anything I'm into."

I ended up sleeping in a van for a few hours before getting up to see Sanka, and then DE$TINYBRINK, who played last. They ended up blowing out the sound system not once but *twice*, ultimately showing that, in many ways, they didn't belong there. Everyone seemed confused by their set, keeping distance from the speakers and the nearly extinguished bon fire, and the guys packed up the van to head back to Tokyo pretty much as soon as they were done. But there was still time to introduce myself to one more person:

"Excuse me, are you DIGITALBOY?"

"Yes . . . "

"Hi, my name is Jillian. You can call me Jill. I research music in Japan, including underground music. I only heard a little bit of your set, but it seemed funny. *Yoroshiku onegai itashimasu.*[5] Bye!"

---

5 Literally, "please [humbly do me the favor of being a part of my life] from now on," but used in situations when you meet someone with whom you might forge a lasting connection; very loosely translatable as "nice to meet you."

The Kero Factory Show in Matsuyama, Ehime prefecture.
Photo by © Copyright Jillian Marshall

A Maid Cafe in Tokyo's Akihabara district:
home to the eponymous girl group AKB48.

The dance procession at the Nishimonai Bon Odori.
Photo by © Copyright Jillian Marshall

Above: Ugo, Akita in the off-season.
Right: With S-san after my first festival in 2015.

Photos by © Copyright Jillian Marshall

Mountains of Akita.
Photo by © Copyright Jillian Marshall

Above: Amerika-town's Statue of Liberty in Osaka; Left: T-shirts for sale in Ame-mura.

Photos by © Copyright Jillian Marshall

Above: Labyrinth and Friendly Giant, DJing sometime in the middle of the night, somewhere in Tokyo. Right: The Mad Scientist at the scene's basement haunt in Tokyo.
Photos by © Copyright Jillian Marshall

Above: High vibes at my "dissertation release" party.

Photos by © Copyright Jillian Marshall

"You Came In Here, Didn't You?"

DURING THE SUMMER OF 2015, I lived in a Chinese-run dormitory in an old-school red-light district in Osaka. Despite the tiny room with walls that didn't quite reach the ceiling, the filthy kitchen with pots and pans covered in black sludge, and the rusted communal shower with garbage in the corner, it was a welcome change of pace from where I had been living in Tokyo for the previous nine months. Named the "Friendship Apartments"—deliciously ironic, considering that most people living there didn't acknowledge one another and one of my neighbors was downright hostile—this run-down share house in a blue-collar neighborhood just south of Shinagawa never felt like home.[1] Along with the crowds, ceaseless rush, rampant consumerism, and isolating anonymity of Tokyo in general, life there spiraled me into a depression that mirrored the dark, damp, cramped living conditions which, no matter how much I cleaned, still felt hopelessly filthy. It took an all-too-necessary month back to the US with friends and family to start feeling like myself again.

---

1 Honestly, the only good part about the Friendship Apartments (other than the relatively convenient location) was that my BFF Lily lived in the apartment above me.

Upon returning to Japan a month later to conclude my fieldwork, my overriding project of self-discovery continued to unfold in new directions. Every day was fresh, lively, and rooted in the present moment. It was a time when I began to see Japan with renewed perspective, going for walks around the neighborhood (which was adorably quaint outside of the red-light district and, to be honest, even within it) while delighting in life's details, remembering that savoring them is what gives life meaning in the first place. It was a time when I leisurely admired the ornate potted plant gardens one can find outside many urban Japanese homes, slowly leafed through vintage magazines from the 1960s in shopping arcades, poked around flower shops to find the most fragrant lilies, took my time selecting ingredients to prepare healthy meals, and frequented the *sentō,* public bath houses, where I repeatedly bumped into, and became friendly with, my madam neighbors (whom I normally saw soliciting customers from their stoops).

It was a time when I hung out with a new group of friends whom I felt like I had known my entire life. Most lived a short train ride to Kyoto away, and with the slower pace of life in western Japan in general we were able to meet several times a week. Sometimes it would be at shows, or at record shops or bars, but we mostly met at The Party House where we cooked, baked, talked, and always listened to music . . . or where I listened to them play synthesizers, anyway.

Sigh

Unsavory gender politics aside, the summer of 2015 was when I first got a glimpse of life truly outside the system: off the socio-cultural grid, and decidedly bohemian. It was a time when we would stay up all night going to the bath houses, playing badminton in a nearby park, listening and dancing to music that DIGITALBOY procured in empty baseball diamonds with portable speakers, and greeting the morning at an old-style breakfast market in an industrial warehouse district north of Kyoto station. A lifelong student in the US, I began to see what life is like without being bound by any convention for the first time, even those that govern health: notably a regular sleep schedule, restraint on substance use, and eating regular meals. And though I had experienced this going to shows in Tokyo, I wasn't there for the behind-the-scenes moments that ultimately create a much more vivid portrait of what "underground" life is all about.

Although I enjoyed spending time with these new and interesting friends, I also relished moments alone when I could observe how my own outlook was changing as a result of these relationships. I suddenly became reacquainted with my creative hobbies for the first time in years, along with an interest in general mysticism (astrology, palm reading, and the like) that I had suppressed during my post-secondary education. So while I will never be the kind of person to stay up all night four times a week, much less doing so smoking and drinking far into the next morning, the underground left its mark on me as I began to live according not to my head, but to my hunches, my instincts, my creativity, my interests, and my heart.

Maybe this is what's lost when we run in the rat race. What's gained when we consider something beyond it.

* * *

A FRIEND WHO LIVED IN A nearby neighborhood where I often browsed for knick-knacks and old books told me that

Osaka is a great city to get to know by bicycle, and generously lent me hers for the summer. During the day I'd ride all over to industrial areas of the city that, through their grit, showed a grounded-ness to a reality that I somehow recognized and felt more comfortable in compared to the air-brushed façade of Tokyo. At night, I'd slowly roll through the neighborhood—after taking a dip at the bath house, of course—with the cool night breeze on my face. I rode smack in the middle of the empty streets, watching the haunting beauty of the quirkily shaped streetlamps cast shadows on the pavement that I knew would later become a nostalgic memory. No matter where I went, I directed myself with intuition—and street signs, yes, but definitely not the internet! As a result, I got to know eastern and central Osaka quite well.

One hot day in August, after writing and relaxing in the dorm all morning, I decided to go for a ride. Left, and another left at that convenience store where I bought magazines with pop stars on the covers that were relevant to my research, and straight past the construction site that might have been abandoned, since no progress ever seemed to be made. Suddenly on the right I noticed a side street I'd never seen before, despite having ridden around the neighborhood many times. The street was appealing, lined with trees and laced with beautiful shadows of sun shimmering through breeze-whipped leaves. Instinctually, I turned onto it and enjoyed what felt like a country road in the middle of the second largest metropolitan area in Japan. After a while, when the sweat was stinging my face and turning my hair into a nest, I looked for a place to turn around when a tiny clothing shop run out of what appeared to be a standalone shack popped up on the left.

An eccentric old lady greeted me and proceeded to show off what she felt were the best pieces. "Very sparkly, yes? I applied the sequins myself!" she boasted, smiling proudly. The shop was lined with racks of the clothes she had altered herself, with one bedazzled shirt more adorably gaudy than the next. A skirt caught my eye, and as I felt the fabric between my fingers I noticed her husband, sitting in the corner and reading a newspaper below a hand-written sign that said *uranai*: fortune telling.

"Wow, do you offer palm reading services?"

"Yes. Would you like to have your palm and birth chart read?"

Hesitating—this type of service can be expensive in Japan—I explained that I might be short on cash, to which he and his wife quickly responded that they would give me a "student discount."

"This is important," they reassured. "Come sit."

The old man asked for the standard information—birth time and place—and proceeded read my chart. Unlike other palm readers I had seen with DIGITALBOY and other friends as kitschy fun, he began speaking to me in great detail about past lives and destiny. Always eager to hear alternative perspectives but healthily skeptical unless convinced according to (an albeit unorthodox version of) logic, I eagerly listened, and followed with a question I felt summed up everything I wanted to know from this interaction, and the Summer of 2015 in general:

"Is destiny real?"

Chuckling, he didn't miss a beat.

"You came in here, didn't you?"

Peripheral Encounters: A Series of Personal/Social/Musical Experiments

Primary Experiment

I. Research question: What would it look like if I brought together my world in Japan with my world in America—the "field" with the home base?

II. Experiment design: Apply for grants and write emails to pretty much every department in the humanities and social sciences on Cornell's campus to get funds for airfare for my Kansai-based Japanese underground musician friends (DIGITALBOY, YOOSK, and Restricted Throw) and to offset venue fees; plan a series of concerts where they perform with my American, classically trained pianist friends.

III. Hypothesis: It will be an important, life-changing, at times uncomfortable, but ultimately rewarding experience for all involved.

Prelude: The Guest Lecture

Suddenly, somehow, the last day of class arrived, which meant that our guests from Japan had also arrived. Yes, the underground DJs were coming to my first-year writing seminar. They'd get the whole class after a few housekeeping details: finishing up final presentations, handing out the final essay assignment, closing remarks. This tour was my gesture of thanks for sharing their world with me in Japan the year before, particularly during the summer of 2015 when I jumped in with two feet and lived the underground lifestyle with them—quite literally during that last month, when I decided to wing it without living arrangements.[1] Bringing the guys to the States using money I wrote dozens of emails and several grant applications to obtain was of academic, ideological, and personal principle. As an ethnographer, this was an experiment with aims to stitch together all of my life-worlds as smoothly as possible through the safe-space of musical performance, the first of which commenced in my class.

They were trying to keep it *so* cool, and it pissed me off a little, to be honest, because there's no way that they weren't a little nervous. After all, they were completely out of their element. Cornell University is a stark departure from underground Japan, where you don't work a "real" job on principle, where you live party to party, sleep all day, stay up all night, and scrounge for the mundane realities of everyday life. But maybe I wanted them to be nervous because I was nervous.

I left it entirely up to the guys to do whatever they wanted for their fifty minutes, save for one duty: to give the students mix CDs that they'd paid for as part of the course materials. Two out of three remembered. The third, whose English is the most fluent, burned his mix CDs in class before taking the reins for the guest lecture . . . *sigh*. But he turned it

---

1   During this time, I crashed with DJ friends who were more than willing to accommodate me (and were very supportive of my choice to "wing it"), and stayed in seedy hotels within my budget when I needed private time.

around when he said, "If you want to understand what we do, we need you to do just one thing. DANCE."

And so, on May 9th, 2016, the Cornell music building hosted its first—and most likely last—Japanese underground DJ dance party.

The Student Center Gig
Cornell University, 5/9/2016

Experiment A

I. Research questions: What is the place of music in society—in this case, music that, according to its makers, needs no explanation and should just be *felt*? How necessary is social media/advertising in generating an audience?

II. Experiment design: Throw an unadvertised dance music party in the student center and see how students react—if they come, if they dance.

III. Hypothesis: A few students from class will show up, and maybe some other people walking by will stop in.

* * *

"Wait, *this* is the student center? I thought it would be outside! But at least there will be beer there, right?"

Um, no. And do you really need a drunk audience?

"You didn't hang up signs?! There's no Facebook event? How is anyone supposed to come??"

Because there will be interesting electronic music blaring from Willard Straight Hall . . .

"You know, this building is a bit too nice . . . can we even play loudly here?"

Would you prefer to play in some smoke-stinking basement at 4am?

"Moving these heavy speakers around campus sure is a lot of work."

So was organizing this entire tour.

* * *

IV.   Results:

They each got to play for forty-five minutes, which is about standard for their shows in Japan. Three students from class showed up, and danced on their own for the full two hours. A lot of students (around twenty) stopped to peer through the doors, listening for a few minutes outside before eventually walking away; given that it was study week, students seemed particularly rushed. Others walked by without a second thought, often wearing headphones or earbuds. The building manager seemed entirely un-phased by the music, which was quite loud and reverberated in the hall. Near the end of the performance, a student—wearing pajamas—wandered in and joined us in dancing. After it was over, he said that this was some of the coolest music he'd ever heard, and asked why there weren't posters or advertising.

The Carriage House Gig,
Ithaca, New York, 5/18/2016

Experiment B

I.   Research questions: See concert program notes below, written by the author.

If you go to Angry Mom records in downtown Ithaca and ask for "classical music," you'll be escorted to the very back of the store to a dusty shelf of unmarked, unsorted boxes. And, if you're patient enough to sift through pops-concert performances of *The Planets*, "best of" albums, and a curiously high volume of Gilbert and Sullivan, you *might* strike gold with a box set of Fauré piano quartets, or John Adams' *Nixon in China*. One could argue that this music doesn't have a large enough following to warrant its own shelf, but then there are entire sections for disco, electronic dance music, noise, grunge, reggae, Native American music, folk, and one shelf just for something called "Weird." What is said about classical music in the US if it remains hidden even in spaces dedicated to obscurity?

If you to go to Japan, Tower Records will have at least two floors dedicated to classical music. The Yamaha sheet music store in Ginza, Tokyo will also have multiple floors of rare, beautifully made scores, many of which cannot be found elsewhere. But dance music? Dancing in public spaces was technically illegal in Japan until 2014 (and rumor has it that the ban might be reinstated). Instead, this music is deep underground, oftentimes literally in that it's performed between the first and last trains in basement music clubs not dissimilar from many new music venues in New York City. Like contemporary/classical music here in the US, it must be actively sought to be found.

Tonight's concert meditates on the hypothesis that classical music is to the US what dance music is to Japan: peripheral, on the edge of society. Classical, contemporary, underground, experimental, countercultural . . . what do these terms actually describe? By programming music that sounds very different yet are treated similarly, we encourage listeners to question the limits of genre, and to perceive similarities over differences. Somewhere in the frontier nestled between the unnecessarily rigid binaries of analog/digital, notated/improvised, classical/underground, and formal/informal, is a clear reminder that music does not sit neatly within the boxes we assign (and not just in record stores).

What happens when you take away the boundaries?

II.   Experiment Design: Convince classical and new music pianist friends from Cornell to play a show with dudes from Japan who DJ and/or make electronic music, and hope for the best.

III.   Program:

    a. R, Liszt transcription of a Schubert song

    b. R, "Uncanny Valley," Nicholas Vines

    c. A, "Fay ce que Voudras," John Zorn

Intermission: Me, first moving away some chairs and then improvising on piano, so as to re-shape the atmosphere into something less formal than the typical "classical music" performance protocol

    d. DIGITALBOY, joining me for a dual improvisation, eventually ventures solo with his own DJ set (he chose to open with a song by Fela Kuti)

    e. YOOSK, playing a Tempest synthesizer (he established danceable beats, and sometimes played as loudly as possible as an apparent act of rebellion)

    f. Restricted Throw, playing his own music (he chose a song he put together that says "fuck" over and over again)

IV.   Hypothesis: As per design, something totally unexpected will happen.

V.   Results:

The concert had good attendance: a mix of graduate students, professors, new music fans, and friends. The atmosphere of the Carriage House—a converted hayloft with warm light, intimate seating close to the stage, and a fully stocked bar with decent wine—accommodated both halves of the program. R, in typical fashion, savored the moment and played what was asked of him, but didn't seem to respond to the second half. A had a large task—take the audience on a trip to outer space, essentially—and executed it well, especially given the time constraint: he re-learned this piece in a matter of weeks, while teaching a writing seminar for undergraduates.[2]

DIGITALBOY wasn't sure how to work the atmosphere, and although Fela Kuti was a logical choice to make in a place like the Carriage House, I was hoping for starker transition into electronica, which didn't come through. YOOSK's set was more in line with my expectations, but since the guys only had around twenty minutes a piece, the effect didn't have the chance to re-establish mood; it felt disconnected. Restricted Throw, who puts together what he calls sound collages rather than playing the music of others like a standard DJ, doesn't improvise or feed off atmosphere: he just pushes play. His song choice reflected a stark unfamiliarity with American social protocol—this was his first time leaving Asia—as well as nerves. About half the audience, including most of the professors, left during the second half. Afterward, the bartender mentioned that he was told this show was going to be "out there," and that it turned out to be even weirder than he had anticipated—but in a good way. He then asked if we were performing together again.

---

2 #PhDlife

Interlude:
The Lot 10 Gig, Ithaca 5/13/2016

THINGS HAVE A WAY OF JUST working out, don't they? I booked this gig for the guys just a few weeks before with no trouble whatsoever, *and* they were going to get paid for it, too.[3] I don't know what kind of sound equipment DJ's/computer musicians/synthesizer players need for a gig, but when we showed up unprepared (without a mixing board), the owner of Lot 10 called his friend and got us one twenty minutes later. There was no official Facebook event or social media presence, but I told all of my friends to tell *their* friends about the awesome party with three underground musicians from Japan.

It was a good-sized crowd, and it got better as the night went on and the dance floor became packed. The audience response was appropriate for each musician: professional dancers vogueing to DIGITALBOY's smooth, disco/deep house set; bouncing and dancing to YOOSK's Tempest synthesizer sounds; jumps and shouts for Restricted Throw's acid house arrangement. Although there were DJs and dancing, it felt much different than parties in Japan. There, perhaps because it's their home turf, the crowd revolves around the DJs, following their every sonic move, trying to talk or flirt with them after the set; if the DJ does something interesting, they shout for him (and it *is* usually "him"). Here, the crowd was interested in itself: friends laughing with and at each other, dancing to impress no one.

The biggest perk of hearing the guys play in the US was being able to dance without being engulfed by the stench of

---

3   This was very good for me, too, since DIGITALBOY came on this trip with only $50 USD . . . with a sizable chunk of it in quarters.

cigarettes. On the other hand, my phone got stolen—which would never happen in Japan.

The ISSUE Project Room Gig
Brooklyn, New York, 5/23/2016

Experiment C

I. Research Questions: Now that we've spent 4,000 dollars securing a venue and piano rental, how can we improve upon the last gig for our New York City debut? In what ways will the other musicians adapt? With (limited) Facebook advertising this time around, who will show up?

II. Experiment Design: Create a Facebook event a few days beforehand and try not to panic over the possibility that no one might show up. Adjust the line-up and the program (see below) to make the transition from classical to underground more smooth and pianism to electronica more stark, and hope for the best.

III. Program:

a. R, Liszt transcription of a Schubert song

b. R, "Uncanny Valley," Nicholas Vines

c. A, "Fay ce que Voudras," John Zorn

d. A, "This is No Less Curious," Louis Chiappetta (2016), New York Premiere

Intermission: with no need to move chairs given the set up in IPR, I waited a few minutes before improvising on piano; S joins briefly for a dual improvisation, eventually fading out for . . .

    e. YOOSK, playing a Tempest synthesizer and immediately establishing a new context. Shouted "DANCE!" at the beginning of his set—which proved very effective.

    f. Restricted Throw, playing his own music (having astutely picked up some basics of American social protocol at this point, he chose a different song; because everyone was already dancing, his music made more sense)

    g. DIGITALBOY, closing this time around so he could observe the atmosphere before jumping in. He ended up playing a song of his own composition off his newly-released EP.

IV.   Hypothesis: As per design, something totally unexpected will happen—but will hopefully go more smoothly than the Carriage House gig?

V.   Results:

A crowd of about twenty people comprised of friends, including friends of the Japanese musicians. The space was beautiful—an entirely empty, slightly dilapidated former train station—and the manager let us use the house sound system free of charge. The piano and electronics reverberated heavily, creating an unexpectedly haunting atmosphere that was quite apropos. Most of the audience stayed for both halves this time around, and they—including two professional dancers—were actually dancing! A friend told me that I am "the weirdest person she knows," which I interpreted as evidence of the show's success at creating something entirely original and absolutely inimitable. The mother, aunt, and godmother of one of the featured composers were in attendance as well, and after the show, the mother congratulated

DIGITALBOY on his set: "That was wonderful. You took me right back to my disco days!"

Experiment Conclusions

- It is indeed possible to utilize university resources to bridge the gap between the field and the academy— although the work certainly doesn't end with the securing of funding.
- In contemporary times, creating internet buzz about performances seems necessary to draw bigger crowds unless people are already aware of the event.
- Putting together a collaborative concert means having to meet various sets of needs. Musicians each have uniquely demanding, sometimes competing needs that are expected to be met with the utmost sensitivity, care, and urgency . . . *i.e.,* We take ourselves just a *wee* bit too seriously.
- To perform in New York City, one needs: a) connections, b) a pre-established reputation, OR c) a venue project manager who is intrigued by your idea and is willing to take a risk on unknowns, as well as d) thousands of dollars, e) organizational skills par excellence, f) patience par excellence. Due to these constraints, it's hard to put together truly experimental programming in New York.
- Performing on piano requires dexterity, flexibility, and ultimately faith that your hands will work well with the instrument provided at your gig.
- Pianos get out of tune by the end of a performance, especially if that performance includes slamming the desk and/or manipulating a Pyrex measuring cup and duct tape on top of the coils.

- DJing or performing electronic music in public venues requires a network of speakers, and a knowledge of how to put them together.
- DJs often work in direct tandem with the atmosphere of the audience, and some feel uncomfortable with instructions of "play whatever you want."
- Was the overall experiment of bringing these two worlds together a success?
  Sure, insofar that the worlds collided.

Coda: Dinner and a Show

WE HAD ARRIVED IN BROOKLYN, FINALLY. Totally frazzled from the tour—the planning, the peace-making, the money spent, the translating, the performance nerves, the anxiety about people showing up—I needed to decompress. And I was upset, because after all of this effort and labor, the guys hadn't yet acknowledged it in a way I could understand.

"*Otsukaresama desu!*"[4] they said to one another, after I struggled to find parking after the harrowing drive to New York from Ithaca. But not to me. And that was a sort of final straw.

Why?! Why can't you just say thank you? My American friends would offer up gratitude in this situation, no questions asked. I don't care what kind of "cultural difference" this might be, or if this is some "underground" thing or WHATEVER. How do you not say thank you?? Ugh, I need to be alone for a little while so I don't kill these fucking man-children.

---

4   As mentioned, this can mean "thanks for all of your hard work"; in other contexts, such as this one, this expression acknowledges effort, spent energy, and general arduousness.

So I told them as much and swiftly strode to the venue, caught up with the pianists, and sat in corner where no one would bother me. As the mood passed and I returned to center, I found myself feeling more charitable. OK, so the guys don't understand American social customs, and they probably never will because Japanese people are socialized into thinking that America is a place where you don't have to be polite—we don't have *keigo*, polite language in English, after all, and unlike the subtle communication used in Japan, we non-Japanese just always blurt out exactly what we're thinking at all times, right? Plus, I'm a woman, and there's no social obligation to acknowledge my active presence and participation in this situation, because only men are considered the primary social actors in Japan.

But, it's my duty both personally and professionally to understand where they're coming from and not take it personally. So. As frustrating as it was to always have to see things from their perspective, where I'm probably a scary, demanding, selfish Medusa beast, it's done. It doesn't matter who is "right" in this situation. After all, I did invite them here, and this was all my idea. Time to move on.

Meanwhile, the pianists and the composer—who were annoyed at my frazzled disorganization, the expense of the tour, and the music they had to play, and regarded the Japanese guys with caustic disdain—were talking about grabbing some dinner before the 7pm start time. Deciding on a cute Italian place around the corner, they headed off. I thought this would be a great opportunity to mend both sides of the equation: the pianists and the DJs, both halves of the show. What if we all ate together? So I set out to find the guys, treat them to dinner, and try to realize my fantasy of all us musicians hanging out together, getting along, and relaxing for the first time since their arrival from Japan.

They were outside taking a smoke break. "Jiru," they said, "thank you for driving us from Ithaca." *Wow,* I thought, *they finally get it! Of course, I feel guilty about having had to ditch them because I was so angry about what I perceived as their total insensitivity, and for probably making them feel more outcasted than they already do, and they're all probably terrified of me at this point anyway, but dinner will be the chance to make everything better!*

We headed to the Italian place to meet the pianists and took a look at the menu. Entrees started at twenty dollars a plate . . . if I treated them, I'd be out *another* hundred dollars which, given the unexpected expenses throughout this entire tour, would just be too much. Too much money, too much stress, too much effort. Again. Sensing my tacit-yet-entirely-obvious stress, and not feeling comfortable in the quasi-fancy atmosphere of the Italian restaurant anyway, they started to fidget, adding, "You know what, there's a bagel joint a few doors down that's more our style."

And then they left.

So there I was, stuck in the middle—specifically, on Court Street in downtown Brooklyn between Queen Italian Restaurant and La Bagel Delight.

Three Akita Bijin

LEGEND HAS IT THAT AKITA PREFECTURE produces more *bijin* than any other prefecture in Japan. No, we're not talking about rice here—although Akita is famous for that, too. We're talking beautiful women: 美 (*bi*, beauty) 人 (*jin*, person).

The Akita Bijin is said to have the palest skin in Japan. She's quite tall—maybe even more robust than the average woman—but in a rustic way that's becoming and wholesome. She's delicate, but sturdy—able to do chores on the farm, perhaps. Her hair is long, dark, and straight, and often worn tied back so she can tend to her work. She's an industrious woman and, with northcountry sensibility, is humble and practical as well. Her eyes are round—soft—and the bridge of her nose a bit taller than her western and southern domestic counterparts. With apple-y cheeks and a warm, yet coy smile, she's down-to-earth holds herself with a quiet dignity that radiates her every move, but never (intentionally) intimidates.

And, perhaps most of all, she is ageless.

S-san

I MET S-SAN WHEN SHE WAS in her early 60's; by now, she must be close to 70. I knew she had to be older, given that she was retired; besides, Japanese women generally age more gracefully than the average American, so I always assume that women are older than they look. But S-san is on a different level altogether. She just looks *so good* for her age.

Her pale face has almost no wrinkles to speak of; her hair, without grays, hangs straight and voluminous at a fashionable length just past her shoulders. If she does wear makeup, it is likely a tasteful sweep of blush across her high cheekbones, and perhaps some mascara to further open up her eyes. She's tall for a Japanese woman, yet she doesn't wear flats. In the summer, her ensemble of a midi-length sundress and wedged sandals is topped off with a straw hat to protect her face from the sun.

S-san is well-known in her community for her volunteer efforts with the blind; she even takes Braille lessons in her free time, in addition to studying English. An adventurous spirit, S-san travelled to New Zealand in her 50s to participate in a home stay program for ten days. She is also a veteran dancer in *Nishimonai*, which she has participated in for thirteen years and counting. Put simply, S-san and her nearly irreverent, quietly glowing independence are a breath of fresh air.

She's not only beautiful, talented, and hardworking, she's also secretly a boss and she totally knows it. I asked how she met her husband—a gentle, quiet farmer—to which she replied: "Lots of men were interested in me, but I knew him for a while and . . . well, he seemed nice and quiet, like he wouldn't bother me too much." She knows she still has it, too: "Jiru-san," she'll coo in her fluttery voice, "I received some strange messages from a few foreign men on Facebook. They all say I'm beautiful. What should I say in response?" She finishes with a giggle.

She's a little pushy sometimes, though perhaps only with me because I am, after all, what's widely regarded in Japan as the helpless foreigner. S-san will remind me of this through closed-mouth giggles if I stumble through a particularly tricky Japanese sentence, or get my head tangled in one of those blasted *noren*.[1] She'll often ask if I know how to use chopsticks, if I can eat raw fish, and other basic skills that some Japanese assume are impossible feats for foreigners. Aware that I'm dealing with an older woman, I let it slide with good humor, and sometimes even play into the role by saying intentionally funny things in Japanese to break the ice.

There has only been one time when I felt she took it too far. After two years of dancing in the festival and rendering them hopelessly tattered, I needed new *tabi,* two-toed socks, and *zouri,* straw sandals. Escorting me to a shop where she knew the owner, she graciously drove me to purchase new pairs of each. In front of the shop keeper, though—who was already bewildered by the sight and prospect of a 6'1" foreign woman shopping for *Nishimonai* dance gear in the first place—she loudly asked: "I wonder what size they'll have . . . you'll have to get men's *tabi* to fit your American feet! *Ne*[2] Jiru-san?"

An indignant rage boiled to the surface. "That's not funny," I snapped. A part of me instantly regretted it; undoubtedly, I shocked her. But on the other hand, forging cross-cultural connection shouldn't be contingent upon being publicly humiliated, all post-colonial politics aside.

What *is* it with this country and my feet?

---

1   *Noren* are curtains put up in doorways to separate the feel between rooms, as well as to create privacy. The curtain theoretically split in two, but merges together close to the the top—right at my face level. Ah, Japan . . . where everything feels miniature if you're above six feet.

2   *Ne:* a grammatical particle in Japanese that seeks agreement.

* * *

AFTER THAT FIRST YEAR OF DANCING, when it was clear that such an arrangement would make more logistical sense, it has become a yearly tradition to stay at S-san's house for a few days before the festival. We use the time to chat and catch up, yes, but mainly to review the dance together. Although the steps are fairly straightforward, there is infinite room to improve upon them—and S-san is widely known in the *Nishimonai* scene as one of the best dancers. To learn from a dancer like her is an opportunity that comes but once in a lifetime, if it even comes at all.

To have been taken on by S-san is a humbling experience—in several senses of the term. After all, there is no room for false praise during our review sessions; now that I know the steps, the real learning can begin. And so I am scrutinized head to toe, movement by movement.

"When you step your leg back, be sure to lift your knee and *ever* so slightly swing your foot *forward* before putting it back into position."

"Keep your head in line with the rest of your torso."

And, of course . . .

"*Mou ichidou:* one more time."

One of the fundamental truths about learning *anything* Japanese, be it the language or the traditional dance, might be that the more someone compliments you, the worse you are. In contrast, being actively critiqued means you are a worthy investment. Although attaining mastery may feel a bit like the endless approach of Xeno's Paradox—or like *Jiro Dreams of Sushi*, for that matter—knowing that you can always make something better is perhaps the biggest lesson of all. In fact, respecting the infinite room to improve upon the dance is, just like the master-apprentice teaching model, as much a part of its aesthetic as the steps themselves.

And so during our annual stay together up in Akita, I happily let S-san boss me around. Plus, if I'm lucky, she divulges her secrets to looking so incredibly young! Apparently, it's *alllll* about the SPF.

N-san

N-SAN IS NEIGHBORS WITH S-SAN, WHERE they live not in Ugo but in the nearby town of Yokote. I'm not sure how long their friendship goes back, but I do know that they've been carpooling to the monthly dance rehearsals for years, and get together for lunches not infrequently.

N-san was in her early or mid-seventies when I first met her. While S-san waltzed up to me during that first rehearsal, N-san only accompanied her because they were riding home together. Later coming to see first-hand that she's much more reserved, I doubt N-san would have come up to the foreigner on her own—but she probably would have capitalized on the opportunity to steal some curious glances.

In a word, N-san is dignified: she holds her coiffed head up high, she moves deliberately, and is always impeccably, practically dressed. What's surprising about her age isn't so much how young she appears, but how healthy and strong she is. Her posture is perfect, and her strong work ethic seems to necessitate ample health to continue her gardening, cooking, and family caretaking. Unlike S-san, she has not spent time abroad and speaks no English. As a result, it seemed to take her some getting used to when S-san started bringing me along in their monthly carpools and lunch dates. While chatting with them in the car, N-san would often not directly respond to me:

"Wow, Jiru-san knows quite a bit of Japanese, doesn't she? Haha!"

Although I wondered if I scared N-san in the beginning—or if perhaps S-san's inclusion of me was somehow unwelcome, or uncomfortable—these insecurities passed when N-san began treating me how I imagine a Japanese grandmother might. I wasn't allowed to pay for meals; N-san picked up the tab for both me *and* S-san. She gifted me with homemade Japanese snacks whenever we'd meet. And her eyes twinkled when she looked at me, often complimenting my appearance and how wonderful it would be if I found a nice Japanese boyfriend . . . peppered, of course, with occasional awe-struck utterances of how *ookii*[3] I am.

It was N-san who got me the major discount on the custom-made *yukata* I wear in the festival. Since she had worked for years at a kimono shop in Yokote, she said it was no problem at all to arrange it. I profusely thanked both women for not only the discount, but for taking me to the kimono shop so I could select which fabric I'd like it made out of. But N-san cleverly brushed it all off, and said with a small smile, sparkling eyes, and a small nod-bow:

"Jiru-san ga odoru no wa taisetsu dakara ne."[4]

N-san is a veteran dancer as well, with at least ten years' experience in the festival. While the taller, perhaps more graceful S-san gets the most snaps from photographers looking to capture beautiful moments, there's a quiet beauty about N-san's dancing. She has an honesty, a frankness, a clarity about her movements that's haunting—even wistful. I

---

3   BIG.

4   "It's important for Jiru-san to dance."

study N-san alongside S-san, and continually learn how the beauty of the dance is naturally expressed differently through every dancer. After all, we bring more to the dance than just our bodies.

As of 2020, I hadn't danced in three years: I took 2018 off because I needed a break from all things Japan following the completion of my dissertation, and in 2019—while cutting my teeth in New York—I couldn't afford to go. And in 2020, there was the coronavirus.

N-san's words, though ring in my ears: "I'm getting older, you know," she told me the last time we danced. She waved away my imminent protests with her hand, while shaking her head. "No, no, it's true. I'm getting older. It's hard on my old body. And I'm not sure how much longer I'll be able to dance."

I listened carefully, with my head slightly bowed. *"Mai toshi, Jiru-san ga odorini kuru no wa taisetsu da yo ne."*[5]

Next year. Next year . . .

O-san

O-SAN LIVES IN THE SAME NEIGHBORHOOD as S-san and N-san. I never spent much time with her; she carpooled with us a few times to dance rehearsals, but mostly drove herself. We had lunch together once with the other ladies, but she didn't end up chatting much with us. Like S-san and N-san, she was a veteran dancer in the festival for years, and danced for all three nights of the holiday every August. During my second and third years, though, she only danced once, and both S-san and N-san seemed slightly confused by her absence.

---

5   "It's important that Jiru-san comes to dance every year."

Naturally, I asked S-san if I was intruding on their circle—
if my presence was somehow making her uncomfortable.
Such a question is pointless, though, because even in the
likely event that I *did* make O-san uncomfortable, S-san
would never tell me. Nevertheless, like in most (Japanese)
social relations, if you have to ask, then your inkling is probably true. I felt sort of guilty about this for a while, until I
realized that I'd done nothing wrong. You can't make
everyone happy, you know?

And that's really all I know about O-san.

Well, that, and it shocked me when I found out that she's a
few years *older* than S-san. Three for three: the legends must
be true.

The Matsuyama Tour

Arrival

"You just think women are treated like dirt here, don't you?"

Um . . . well, yes.

I TOOK THE TRAIN BECAUSE I knew what the road trip with the Kansai DJs down from Kyoto would look like. They'd control the music the entire way, without thinking of asking if there was something I might like to hear. They'd stop for frequent bathroom breaks, but only so that they could smoke: a habit on which Americans and Japanese take a different socio-cultural stance. There'd be no effort to include me in conversations, and so instead I'd have to sit quietly and wait for my turn to be included in the game of double-dutch that is Japanese social interaction: observe, see the pace, get ready, jump in—and jump out once you sense that your time is up.

It's not because they're rude; it's because they're Japanese men. They are deciding what everyone should do because that's what's been decided that *they* should do.

Japanese social structure is top-down, meaning that the guy (and it is 99.9% of the time a guy) occupying the highest spot in the hierarchy exclusively takes the reins. Everyone must treat this person with unequivocal respect, and defer to him in any way possible.[1] He gets to decide when to stop, what music to listen to, when and what we eat, how long the smoke break is, if we should take a scenic detour, if we stop at an electronics junk shop along the way, the topics of conversation . . . everything. There's no room for any discussion or compromise, either, as it would cause the hierarchy to implode. It'd be chaos, anarchy—with no rules in place, no one would know how to behave.

So since I had the Japan Rail Pass and it was going to be free anyway, I opted to ride a series of trains down for my last bit of alone time for the next week, and met up with the guys at Matsuyama station. Immediately, the group decided to stop at a hot spring to refresh their energies. I'd normally welcome this proposition, except that it was too early. My hair has a particular routine and I didn't want to show up to the house with sopping curls and no makeup,[2] but at the same time, I didn't want to upset anyone by being a spoilsport . . . even though no one asked me if I had wanted to go in the first place.

I was a little on edge that evening to begin with since, as a foreigner, meeting new groups of Japanese people can be

---

1   And the more creatively deferential you become, the more polite (and feminine) you're considered. Not that this isn't a useful lesson to learn, particularly for those of us brought up in America and other western societies where humility seems like an afterthought or bonus, but not a priority.

2   It seems that wearing makeup in Japan is actually something of a social courtesy. From observation, the majority of Japanese women wear at least some (and many wear a lot), and it's considered shocking and lewd to be seen applying it in public (like in a train) because the illusion is spoiled.

stressful. Like the *Hunger Games*, your fate is decided in a moment—in this case when the Japanese people decide if they should talk to you normally, like you're a child, or in self-conscious English that prevents real conversation from happening. There's also that crucial initial few minutes when you assess where you belong in the hierarchy. Would this the kind of group where I'd have to insert myself at the very bottom to show that I understand how these things work in Japan/that they don't have to be afraid of me, or is this a more cosmopolitan crowd that's going to treat me like a regular person from the get-go? How polite will I have to be? Do I have to use *masu/desu* or is plain form verb use acceptable?[3]

What ended up happening was that I was left out of the hierarchy establishment entirely. In fact, it was the worst-case scenario where not even the person sitting next to me initiated conversation, thus rendering me part-less as everyone else settled comfortably into their roles. When it was time to start grilling, all the women jumped up to get meat, veggies, seafood, and more beer for the guys. Desperate to feel like part of the group, I offered to help, but they told me to stay seated because I was "the guest."

So there I was, sitting with these dudes who were doing what Japanese dudes do—performing their role according to the established hierarchy—and were thus lavishing each other with the appropriate level of attention, while ignoring

---

3   Verbs in Japan are conjugated according to levels of politeness, the expectations of which change depending on where you are on the hierarchy. *Masu/desu* is a safe bet if you want to be polite, but that same politeness often creates a distance between potential friends that can make it more difficult to actually get to know someone, and develop trust.

the lowest two rungs on the ladder. Yep, me. The a) female b) foreigner. The ordering here is important, because if I were a *male* foreigner, they would have showered me with beer, been the first to offer me the tastiest items fresh off the barbecue, asked me questions, laughed at all my jokes even if none of them are actually funny, and treated me like the smartest, most interesting, most attractive person in the room.

Not that I would want that, at all. That kind of treatment is even more exclusionary, as it is entirely illusory, saccharine, fake. But as a woman—and the blonde-haired foreigner in the room a foot taller than anyone else there— I ended up sitting there quietly, wishing that this interaction could be more natural, and becoming increasingly aware of how awkward it was that I *still* hadn't said anything. Excluded though I was, I could also strongly sense that everyone was wondering why I wasn't participating, perhaps because foreigners are stereotyped as unwitting comedic relief, the scapegoat, laughably blind to the delicate balance of Japanese social relations: "Haha, I've got a funny story about ME relevant to this topic!" Not wanting to play the last-ditch role of the foreign minstrel, however, I sat silently in a mix of sadness, confusion, resentfulness, and a deep sense of shame.

What did I do wrong?

It seemed that the best choice would be to excuse myself when I felt tears welling up, so that's what I did. I didn't want to embarrass myself any further, or worse, the friends who had brought me there.

All of You

"Yeah, this is my favorite record of hers. It's really awesome, super smooth, especially the B side. We should listen to this one."

Thanks for the . . . approval?

WELL, THAT'S ACTUALLY SLIGHTLY OUT OF context. It went more like this:

"Hey, Jiru-chan, you brought vinyl with you? Are you doing a show?"

"I don't have special plans, but if there is an opportunity . . . "

"Wow, these look pretty interesting. What kind of music is this?"

"I have all kinds. This one (*The Golden Age of Benny Goodman*) is 1930s swing jazz, analog dance music. It's super fun."

"How about this one?" Charles Ives, *The Concord Sonata*, played by John Fitzpatrick.

"This is . . . a sort of crazy piano piece written by an insurance salesmen/composer who wrote music with . . . sudden transitions. He'll write a beautiful melody and then (splitting hand gesture) poof!"

"Sounds cool. Let's put it on!"

"Ummmm well, actually, you may not like it, it may not match your ears . . ."

"Yeah, yeah, that one's kind of . . . yeah, let's not listen to it."

Hey, YOU don't get to say that about my music . . .

"OK, well, how about this one?" Ahmad Jamal, *All of You*.

"Oh, I love this! He's a jazz pianist from the 1950's. It's—"

"Yeah, this is my favorite record of hers. It's really awesome, super smooth, especially the B side. We should listen to this one."

You haven't asked once about the records that you've seen me hauling around for weeks, let alone set up an opportunity for me to play anywhere like I did for you when I brought you to the States. This is the first time anyone's asked about MY music the entire time I've been here, and yet you STILL found a way to make it about YOU.

Thanks for the . . . approval?

We listened to the record, but I couldn't enjoy it. It was no longer mine; instead, it was a reflection of his *sasuga* (just like him, as always, true to form)[4] "good taste."

Exit, Act 1 of Many

"Can't you see that I'm working for my show? Don't you ever think about anyone but yourself?!"

That's funny, because I feel the same way. Is playing around on a synthesizer really more important than the fact that I came across the planet to be here with you?

Is one of us right, or are we actually both wrong?

The Kero Factory Show

I OPTED FOR A CAB FROM the *ryokan* Japanese-style inn I was hooked up with in Dōgo, downtown Matsuyama, right next to all the famous hot springs and the cute *shōtengai* arcades selling local knick-knacks. I couldn't stay with him anymore, waiting for him to come upstairs after drinking

---

4 Interestingly, *sasuga* can also imply just the opposite. The word is a delicious example of how the Japanese language is ripe with opportunities to say something quite scathing while totally covering your tracks.

and smoking all night with his friends, and then sleeping all day while I twiddled my thumbs. After the last fight, I needed to get away from him—from everyone.

When we pulled up to the bar five minutes later, I was relieved to know that the show was within walking distance. Even though I've been going to these parties for years, pulling an all-nighter is still hard. There's a part of me that just doesn't see the point of it. Why do we have to do this at night? Is this just some masochistic routine that everyone is actually enjoying? Every so often is fine, but to do this consistently? I mean, what about the next day? Besides, if I don't sleep, I'm like a bear who hasn't hibernated long enough.

I like to have an escape route.

I didn't go to the show the night before because I was still too upset about everything, about coming down to Matsuyama for this stupid tour in the first place. And apparently, he was wrecked by the fact that I really didn't show up to his gig after all. Our friends were pushed to their limits, probably thinking that I'm just some crazy American girl who can't control her emotions and is downright masterful at ruining their harmless fun, but on the other hand admissive of the fact that he can be astoundingly insensitive, that I did come all the way here, and that he's not exactly the portrait of stability himself . . .

It was all just too much. The whole thing felt destroyed beyond repair.

But sometime early on the next evening, after wondering what to do, if I should just go back to Tokyo and call it quits, something changed . . .

What if I just enjoyed myself for the rest of the time on this trip?

What were any of those fights really about, anyway? Is it possible that this has all been one giant cultural misunderstanding? Besides, I have a relationship to Japan independent of all this stuff, and I worked hard to come here. And I loved going to shows since before I met any of these people, and nothing's going to change that. I'm going to make the most of this time, hear some music that I can't hear back in the US, enjoy these people for who they are, let go, and just be in this moment.

When I walked in, everyone seemed surprised—nervous if I was going to cause another emotional scene, perhaps, but also happy . . . ? Anyway, there were smiles, hugs.

"You made it!"

"You're the researcher, right? I heard you were in town! Let's have a drink and talk!"

"Wait, *you're* the researcher? Can we take a picture together?"

Yes. Feeling good.

Nursing a tequila shot, I soaked up the scene. What's underground Shikoku, the smallest and arguably most socially isolated of Japan's four main islands,[5] feel like?

A cozy, intimate basement space with a black-and-white checked linoleum floor. Low lights, an unironic disco ball. Older Japanese people with beards and dreadlocks who really vibe reggae and dub. Smiles, laughs, a refreshingly distinct lack of pretension. A DJ booth in the corner with a decent sound system and a small bar in the opposite corner. Mirrors for walls, with two standing tables against one, a couch against another. Above the DJ gear, a poster with three Black soul singers from the 1970s that echoes a different time, one when people connected over beautiful, fresh,

---

5   Just ask Ōe Kenzaburo: the prize-winning author whose complicated relationship with his Shikoku roots informs many of his books.

funky, empowering music from the heart, when people got together, when people smiled, when there were no selfies or social media to distract from the now, when people were free, looking for real love, and danced.

So that's what we did.

(And yes, I walked back to my inn, but not until the party had ended the next morning.)

The Matsuyama Beer Festival Show

The guys went with Miso-chan; I went with Mae-chan. They had to get there a little earlier to set up their gear, and we wanted to take our time getting dressed. Mae-chan's undupli-cable sense of style lead her, after much deliberation, to wear a t-shirt emblazoned with a graphic of Old Crow whiskey. It's a deliciously bold choice, not least because of its tomboy charm, but also because Japanese society's emphasis on appearance lends a particular importance to fashion. Indeed, this is one of my favorite parts about everyday life in Japan, where my somewhat wacky sense of balance is comparatively understood, perhaps even appreciated in a way that it can't be in American society. So, feeling good that day and excited to see the guys play an outside, casual set at the Matsuyama Beer Festival, I opted for something more adventurous: an item I found right before coming on this trip that I wanted to bust out on a special occasion, when I was feeling especially confident.

After all, there's no other way to wear an oversized, hot pink romper from the 1980s except with total, unwavering belief that you can pull it off.

So obviously I stood out, and because I stick out anyway—and since Matsuyama is a town with almost no foreign presence to speak of, save for a small community of English teachers—all eyes were on me. And on this particular day, I really didn't care.

I know, I know, I get it, I'm fundamentally different, I'll never be one of you people or, you know, human or whatever, so I might as well just stick out as much as possible and give you what you want. Eat your heart out, because here comes an actual pink elephant!

The guys were getting synthesizers, laptops, and tablets ready for their gig in about an hour. After sampling local brews from around Shikoku and enjoying the un-duplicable festivity of Japanese day drinking,[6] we wandered over to say hi.

However, we were quickly intercepted.

"Hello! Hello! Very beautiful. Where you from?"

Ugh, really? I don't have energy for this. Time to fall back on the classic routine.

"Sorry, I don't speak English."

"*A re? Eigo de hanashiteiru! Nihongo ga hanaseru?* (Huh? You're speaking in English! Do you speak Japanese?)"

"*Nihongo ga wakarimasen.* (I don't understand Japanese.)"

"*A re??* (HUH??)"

And I walked away.

Flabbergasted, this guy clearly didn't get the hint and instead joined the guys, who were watching this go down with unbridled amusement. He sits down with them on some milk crates and starts asking questions: Who is she? Where is she from? How do you know her? Does she have a boyfriend? However, the guys play along with this and actually answer his questions—including the last one—which leaves me a bit confused. Are

---

6   Perhaps because Japan doesn't have any open container laws, and because drinking in public places during the daytime is far more socially acceptable than it is in the US, celebrations ranging from outdoor festivals to cherry blossom viewing often prominently feature alcohol as a central node in the activities. It's fun, liberating, and feels delightfully rebellious, like getting tipsy with your parents.

they flirting with him on my behalf or something? Why aren't they just telling him to go away? Is this not considered a gross infringement of boundaries in Japan? I basically told this creep to get lost, so why has he elected to further invade my social space? Does he not think I'm serious? Are this total stranger's feelings more important to my friends than mine?

Taking matters into my own hands, I turned around and marched up to this broseph.

"Hey, what are you still doing here? Why are you talking to my friends?"

The guys burst out laughing. I'm sure I broke dozens of social taboos in an instant, but I didn't care. It's not like I yelled at him or hit him or did anything else that would be clearly inappropriate; I was just standing up for myself. Besides, why is the *man* here allowed to push social limits, but not the *woman*? For this particular situation, I made the snap decision that I didn't actually mind reinforcing the crippling stereotype that American women are "aggressive" compared to Japanese women. And the guys were loving every minute of this. Apparently, so did this dude, who looked at me with an expression of fear, yes, but also lust, disbelief, and utter amazement.

Naturally, I was rendered even more disgusted. What's it take for a guy to back off in this country? Leave me alone, the purpose of my existence is most certainly not to function as an ideal accessory for male social interactions! That's when Mae-chan grabbed me by the arm and escorted me away, laughing, but reminding me:

"Jiru, Jiru . . . we girls don't do that in Japan."

Why not?

初*DJ* の経験[1]

Experiment:
Testing the Aesthetic Limits of the
Japanese Underground
January 5th, 2017
Western Shibuya-ku, Tokyo
Personnel (in order of performance):
N, B, W (author), Labyrinth, Friendly Giant

I.   Research questions:

Although the underground is generally understood as the site of (Japanese) society's most experimental music-making, why do most people opt to play electronic- or synthesizer-derived sounds? And if dance music is inherently countercultural in Japan due to the anti-dance law and the general conformist pressures of Japanese society, how might non-electronic dance music be received? What would happen if someone played music not generally recognized as "cool"?

II.   Experiment design:

Put together a show at the last minute at the basement hole-in-the-wall club. Make no social media flyers and

---

1   *Hatsu DJ no keiken:* "[My] First Experience DJ-ing"

create a set list comprised of whoever can show up in my circle of Tokyo-based DJ friends, and play selections from my vinyl collection—which is music not widely understood as "cool" and includes almost no electronica.

III. Hypothesis: Not sure, but hopefully people a) show up and b) dance.

IV. Results:

Three DJ friends performed, one flaked at the last minute. The owner of the club also played a set. Most of the people I invited (the day of the show, classic me) showed up; my faithful and beloved best friend Lily also came to the show with an acquaintance and stayed all the way until first train, even though underground music isn't exactly their cup of tea. We started the evening with a celebratory beer for the New Year, and my Japanese friends heartily narrated the *kanpai* toast with a moving *okaerinasai*: "Welcome back [to Japan]."

N and Labyrinth showed me how to use the turntables (which I had never touched before in my life) and the set was punctuated with cheers of encouragement. Friendly Giant posted live play-by-play updates of my set on Instagram, while Labyrinth and B posted videos to both Instagram and Twitter. One of Friendly Giant's captions read, "W is born!" The profundity of this support made me understand the centrality of the underground social space to these musicians—that this is the center of the world, and identity is constructed around and by it. While Labyrinth and N took naps at various points in my nearly two-hour set, everyone else danced and responded otherwise to the music I played, not all of which is overtly danceable. Almost none of my selections were recognized by the audience; Labyrinth and Friendly Giant were impressed that only two of my selections came up on the song identification app Shazam, while B said that she'd never before seen a DJ show like mine. A friend said that hearing and seeing my DJ set felt like she was watching me listen to music alone in my room.

Success! Intent realized!

Experiment Conclusions

DJING FOR NEARLY TWO HOURS FLEW by with swift bliss, like a good night's sleep where nine hours feels like twenty minutes. The feeling of having people cheer and dance to music that means so much to you—songs that put a smile on your face even when you hate everything (Benny Goodman, "Down South Camp Meeting"), that are drippingly sensual without objectifying/degrading women in any way whatsoever (Ahmad Jamal, "All of You"), that you know will incite a reaction (Yoko Ono, "Kiss Kiss Kiss"), that will confuse everyone but are worth taking that risk for (Charles Ives, "The Alcotts" from the *Concord Sonata*)—is extremely empowering, and downright energizing (Even at 3am!). As a DJ, you're in control of the room's atmosphere and have the power to get everyone dancing, and ultimately make everyone happy, by sharing your music—by being one of the most intimate incarnations of yourself. Immediately after finishing, I started mentally assembling a set list for my next show, packed with music that, though not "dance" music, I know can get people dancing!

Further Conclusions

YOU KNOW WHO YOUR FRIENDS ARE by who comes to your show.

Other notable selections from the *Hatsu* DJ set:

- Queen, "Fun It"
- Kanye West, "Champion" and "Flashing Lights" (a eulogy of sorts for pre-*Life of Pablo* Kanye)
- Supertramp, "Goodbye Stranger"
- Sun Ra, "Dance of the Cosmo Aliens"
- The Doors, "LA Woman"
- Fats Waller, "African Ripples"

Interlude II: Music for the People!

The following is an actual blog post I wrote for MTV and the Fulbright Foundation's joint fellowship program for music research, published in the late winter of 2015. The fellowship doesn't exist anymore because the only requirement—keeping a blog—wasn't met by too many of the recent fellows. Great job, everyone!

* * *

Fulbright mtvU Fellows
Jillian Marshall – Japan

So Close, Yet So Far: J-pop, Consumerism, and Alienation?
I glanced at my clock. Ten o'clock on the nose. Perfect. I'll wait a few minutes just in case the website is slow. I smiled. After missing other shows and waiting too late to buy tickets, I've finally and totally got this one.

At 10:35am, after countless website crashes and error messages, I finally made it to the Tokyo Dome ticket center web page for Haru Fest 2015 headlined by Kyary Pamyu Pamyu—one of Japan's most famous pop stars domestically and, recently, overseas—and was informed that the show had already been sold out, not even an hour after ticket sales were opened.

Keep in mind that Tokyo Dome has 55,000 seats.

These true-to-fact anecdotes reveal an important angle of the interesting paradox in Japanese popular music culture: it boasts to be for and of Japan. In terms of this music being "for" the people, J-pop stars—much like American pop stars—often gush about how appreciative they are of the fans, which creates the potential to form emotive bonds with these musicians without having to actually meet them in the flesh. Kyary Pamyu Pamyu often uses social media, especially her Twitter account, to let the world know about what she's up to, often posting pictures of her latest photo shoots or thanking fans for remembering her birthday. Social media is especially adept at creating a (false?) sense of intimacy because, while the Internet offers everyone a voice, it comes with the price tag of personal, human identity; some may disagree with me on this point, but the web is, at the end of the day, an anonymous space that functions as an *imagined*, rather than *material*, reality.

In any case, many of Kyary's fans are foreign, as she has become popular around the globe with what many perceive to be her . . . well, stereotypical "Japanese-ness." American pop culture blogger Perez Hilton featured her 2012 music video for *CANDY CANDY* on his site with the caption, "This video is ridiculous . . . but we love it so!" It's worth noting that Kyary's musical output isn't especially prolific—she releases one album a year, capping her discography at three—but her face is everywhere around Tokyo in billboards, commercials, train advertisements . . .

AKB48, an idol group which has taken Japan by storm since their debut in 2005, informs and praises fans through more formal media outlets. In fact, AKB48 has their own weekly newspaper, which you can buy next to the Asahi Shinbun—the Japanese equivalent of the New York Times—at any convenience store. The group was created by Akimoto Yasushi, who envisioned the group as "idols you could meet": a highly democratic musical act that would allow fans actually to interact with the members not just through daily performances, but through annual voting processes that rank the members of the group in terms of overall appeal (which, itself, is based on many factors, including looks, humility, hard work, and other attributes ascribed to ideal femininity— and, save for looks, citizenship—in Japan).

To this end, a special magazine is published every year with the election results, and features interviews with the top members. Akimoto's 48-member idol group template proved so successful that the AKB48 brand has expanded to comprise a school of aspiring idols organized, who generally take on the task of performing daily in Akihabara (there would be mayhem in Akihabara if the primary 48 members did live shows every day). Additionally, other 48-groups across the country and other parts of Asia have been created that are supposed to represent these regions, including HKT48 for the city of Hakata, NMB48 for the Namba district of Osaka, SKE48 for the Sakae district of Nagoya, and JKT48 for Jakarta, Indonesia.

What these rather staggering realities illustrate is that, while J-pop is marketed as the music of and for Japan, it's actually incredibly difficult to access. This leads me to wonder what Japanese popular culture—and perhaps popular culture anywhere—actually reflects and represents. For example, it's quite ironic that AKB48 was designed to encourage maximum contact between the performers and their fans, but seats at the shows featuring the top 48 members are nearly impossible to snag. It's also hard to believe that Kyary Pamyu Pamyu sings music for the masses when seats for her (one!) concert this entire spring are sold out within minutes; this is especially pronounced when my favorite underground musicians—who are also friends and acquaintances—perform up to three times a week in venues where there is no separation whatsoever between the musicians and the listeners.

So if popular music in Japan is so hard to hear live and is often rarely performed, how are fans actually exposed and encouraged to interact with this music?

Kyary hasn't released any new songs or videos since I've come to Japan, but I can easily think of several products she's endorsed. While AKB48 is more prolific—after dropping singles for months, they just released their sixth album in full on January 21st of this year—the AKB48 Cafe and Shop, as well as the AKB48-themed slot machine parlors scattered throughout the Tokyo metropolis, speak for themselves. People are encouraged to consume music not just through a 3-minute long, heavily engineered song written by men in swanky offices (specifically Nakata Yasutaka writing for Kyary, and Akimoto writing for AKB48) and performed by these young women—itself a strong commentary on gender relations. We are encouraged—perhaps primarily—to interact with these musicians through consuming their products and whatever products they endorse.

This leaves me with a few questions about what Japanese popular music says about contemporary Japanese society. Life in Tokyo can be quite alienating, precisely because it is so unfathomably huge. Like New York, Tokyo never sleeps. The trains are packed at all hours of the day with men (and some women) in business suits, many of whom work *zangyou* (uncompensated overtime) late into the night. On a more somber note, trains are often delayed due to *jinshin-jikou*, which translates as "human body incident" . . . which more often than not indicates a suicide. The apartments are *small*, and even though personal space is a rarity here (although I have read that Americans require more personal space than people of any other society in the world, so who am I to judge?), it's easy to feel alone when everyone is glued to their smart phone. And anyway, Japanese society doesn't exactly condone small talk about the weather with strangers. It seems like people here are always in a hurry to get somewhere, and one can easily feel, at times, lost in what is indeed a ceaseless, churning sea of people, trains, sirens, cars, bicycles . . .

It strikes me that, every time I go to Akihabara around 4:30, the crowd of people standing outside the AKB48 Cafe and Shop don't look especially exuberant; the group looks somewhat sheepish, in fact, and people keep rigidly to themselves. I grabbed lunch in the AKB48 Cafe a few months ago, and most people were there by themselves as well, eating in silence while ogling pictures of teenage girls. I can't help but notice that this is in striking contrast to the deep sense of community that runs through the underground and traditional music scenes here in Japan.

Of course, I'm reserving personal judgment. Instead, I'll continue to keep my eyes (and ears) open, and trying to make sense of what members of each musical community—traditional, popular, and underground—have in common with one another, as well as with members of the other scenes. Maybe, if I can actually manage to get tickets to a show (boy, have I tried; yes, this is part of the experience; and yes, it *will* happen!), I'll see a different kind of community emerge.[1]

* * *

MY ORIGINAL BLOGPOST RECEIVED THREE COMMENTS, quoted verbatim:

> "I have found this post very insightful and the style of writing exceptional, Thank you for posting."

> "Very insightful analysis of Kyary Pamyu Pamyu and AKB48 in terms of relating them to consumerist culture— I'd be very interested to hear more about why this particular style is of such appeal and popularity in Tokyo. How does it resonate with the citizens' culture?"

> "So, yoir idea of getting Fix and Flip Loanhs really serve great and it makes a very useful investment on things that are considered to bbe all effective and widespread. You have to keedp in mind that your future prosperity depends on a right selection of property and tthe fair kind of fixation. s training, I am purchasing 2 large multi ffamily projects, with no money outt of my pocket, plus I'm developing a solid income by prdoviding financing to investors looking to do the same. Sometimes a house is extremely nice and attractive but you can't buy it only due to its bad suburbs. Quantity borrowed varies from client to client on different groups of resources."

---

1 I never did nab tickets to an arena show. Instead of framing this as some kind of ethnographic failure, I understood this result as a reflection of the popular music world itself. Lord, how I tried . . .

On Making it Big

SOON AFTER I STARTED GOING TO all of their shows, it was clear that DE$TINYBRINK was getting hot. Their charisma was off the charts. With a square, pulsating, raw beat of the drum machine rooting the post-apocalyptic, explosive, post-industrial blast-off of the synthesizer, DE$TINYBRINK were so Tokyo, so now—and they knew it. The room felt electric whenever the Mad Scientist walked in, and if DE$TINYBRINK played a show, you were in for a good time.

By the spring of 2015, they had even started touring in Osaka and Kyoto. Since I happened to be in town at the same time catching some other shows, I decided to check them out in a new setting. They played at two clubs that I later realized were not equivalently underground spaces to where they gigged in Tokyo, but were more mainstream venues that hosted bigger artists. That's when it occurred to me that DE$TINYBRINK was one of the bigger artists, not least because they were from Tokyo—widely considered the most cosmopolitan city in Japan—but because they were legit getting popular.

It was also around this time that I noticed how DE$TINYBRINK really only had one style: an hour-plus long performance that started slow, maybe with some melodies etched out by the synthesizer, while a foundational beat was gradually mixed in until the whole thing exploded into a relentless, noise-y interstellar time-warp that tapered off into a coda of post-coital melodic utterances. But at their gig in Osaka's Compufunk Records in April of 2015, they tried something new with a slower set seemingly influenced by a forced interpretation of modal jazz.[1] Needless to say, the energy in the room stalled; what they played wasn't terrible, but it lacked context following the explosive momentum of their first set. And from my perspective, after having seen almost every show over the course of seven months, it just didn't suit them at all.

Uh, wtf is this?

That's when it occurred to me that, by expanding their repertoire, the group was trying to expand their audience. This led to a host of new questions: what, exactly, is DE$TINYBRINK all about? Is their sound a natural expression of the group's musical sensibilities, or is it calculated to garner popularity? By this point, I had already begun meditating on the underground music world's relationship to success. On the one hand, the underground boasts a counterculture of radical self-expression and being "anti-system"; on the other, Tokyo is a hard place to be a starving artist. Taking the train home at 5am after their more recent shows, I often wondered what would happen if DE$TINYBRINK made it big.

---

1 Although modal jazz never factored into their sound, the group's inspirations, among many grunge/industrial groups from LA and Europe (namely Robe Door and Empty Set), included the highly underrated jazz legend Sun Ra and his Intergalactic Myth Science Solar Arkestra. These influences came through in concept, but not in feeling, during this particular performance.

Was the whole point of the underground to eventually leave?

The Mad Scientist, who made all the group's decisions, was notoriously hot-headed and difficult to get along with.[2] A self-described "drifter," he grew up with well-to-do parents in Tokyo and Tsukuba, a city in nearby Ibaraki prefecture where his father worked at the local university. He said that all of the other kids were "sons and daughters of, like, astronauts" and that he struggled with feelings of guilt about having such materially successful, supportive parents, *and* a strong interest in counterculture. After finding himself unable to collaborate with band mates in Japan long-term— one Facebook photo he uploaded showed him playing a synthesizer with the caption "You know only non-human won't leave your band"—he followed his rebellious streak to Europe and Los Angeles.

Abroad, he gigged around as a bass guitarist in several bands[3]—even playing at South By Southwest in Austin, Texas one year—and felt more musically and personally accepted than he ever did in Japan. After returning to Tokyo in 2014, equipped with these international musical experiences, he put together his latest brainchild with a long-time friend and lone surviving potential band mate, Mr. Drum Machine. Thus was DE$TINYBRINK born.

By June of 2015, they were officially on the radar as the headliners at Liquidroom: one of Tokyo's biggest clubs. It was certainly exciting to see DE$TINYBRINK connect with so many people, and to see a large audiences of more normative

---

2   A musician that used to play with the Mad Scientist once confided to me: "As a bandmate and a person, he's kind of . . . difficult. But as a musician he just has that certain *je ne sais qua, so . . . we deal with it, you know?*"

3   Including such unforgettable names as "Topping Bottoms" and "DJ Dog Dick."

Japanese people vibe to the down-and-dirty, raw and unfiltered vision of Tokyo that was their music. Yet, a part of me grieved as I joined an audience comprised of hundreds of people. Although I spoke with them after the set and received a discounted entry fee thanks to Mr. Drum Machine, part of this evolution felt like a betrayal—as though those of us who had supported them along the way became secondary to the "masses" of which we were now a part. I couldn't help but wonder: given the Mad Scientist's inconsistent musical history, maybe their objective was never about community, connection, and the joy of music-making in the first place. After all, it's not like he was a particularly humble or grateful dude who showed any real interest in anyone but himself. DE$TINYBRINK's evolution seemed deliberate, perhaps even strategic . . . which is probably why I wasn't happier for them.

It wasn't just me who seemed to have these inklings. Etched in my memory is the image of DJ Edamame, who had since become a supporting act in the scene, looking on at DE$TINYBRINK from backstage. His stance—leaning against a pole motionless yet entirely focused, his chin resting on a clenched fist as he gazed in DE$TINYBRINK's direction but seemingly beyond them—belied a mix of regret, bitterness, resentment, and defeat. Because for as disagreeable as the Mad Scientist could be, DE$TINYBRINK really did just have a certain *something* about them that couldn't be defined, much less contained. And maybe that's why they were headlining at Liquidroom, and why Edamame was working backstage as a side gig.

A few months later, DE$TINYBRINK catastrophically broke up when it was revealed that the Mad Scientist was a petty thug. It turns out that he had been using the people and places of the scene for his own advancement, and was beat up in a dramatic fistfight and cast into exile: never again to set foot in the club where he and Mr. Drum Machine had begun recording their first vinyl release, and where I had heard them play so many times. Today, Mr. Drum Machine continues to perform solo and with a new group formed after the irreparable dissolution of DE$TINYBRINK.

Funny how things work out, isn't it?

DJ Edamame, by the way, continues to do very well for himself.

And . . . I want to get my paws on that vinyl more than even an original pressing of Taeko Ohnuki's *Sunshower.*

Akita-ben

Akita, *as in Akita prefecture; ben, meaning dialect when used as a suffix but "poop" when used on its own—a lesson I learned the hard way.*

JAPANESE IS ONE OF THOSE LANGUAGES, like Latin, that contains seemingly countless possibilities to conjugate a single verb. It's mind-boggling, and unless proven otherwise, I maintain that teachers of both languages must derive some sort of pleasure from confusing students on exams. Hey, gotta weed them out somehow, right? Unfortunately, this doesn't include the diehard students in most Japanese language classes: Americans who really wish they were either anime characters, samurai warriors, ninjas, or all three. This isn't to say that taking Japanese isn't fun, per se, but with so much of energy dedicated to remembering how to say something, *anything*, with 100% correct grammar—while staring off death stares from Sailor Moon in the process— the process of learning to speak coherently renders many non-native Japanese speakers exhausted, to say the least. On top of that, verbs are conjugated according to politeness to such extremes that the honor- and humblerifics (and yes, "humblerifics" is a real thing) are essentially separate languages altogether. Even Japanese people admit, sighing, that they can *never* remember how to say it in *son-keigo* (the highest form of politeness, except for whatever it is you use when talking to the emperor).

Basically, if you make a mistake, you sound both stupid *and* rude.

The grand irony of it all is that you're taught the driest, most formal, polite, distance-creating forms of the language in the classroom that you a) basically would never use anyway, except b) if you don't have any friends. So, perhaps like any language, the best way to learn Japanese is to go to where it's spoken and get a feel for it. When I first moved to Japan in 2009, after having only half-heartedly studied the language for a year, I picked things up quickly out of sheer necessity: living on a rural island nestled between Shikoku and the mainland, it was the only option. Not only that, but I ended up learning what's considered an *inaka-kusai* ("stinking of the countryside") form of Japanese that, while forging a certain degree of immediate intimacy with Japanese people due to sheer novelty ("Haha! She sounds like an old fisherman!"), later proved problematic in getting taken seriously.

Upon matriculating graduate school two years later, the Cornell Japanese Department had a hard time placing me in a class: "She speaks with fluency and has an ability to communicate what she wants to say, but this verb conjugation chart is all over the map; these are first-year mistakes. Her vocabulary is nuanced and practical, but it's unpolished, informal. And what's with the Kansai-ben??"[1] However after

---

1   The dialect and stress used in western Japan: Osaka and Kyoto, along with Hyogo, Wakayama, and Mie prefectures.

two years of courses and a summer of intensive study, my Japanese was finally "fixed." I was well-prepared to move to Japan again, this time in Tokyo, to undertake formal research.

While I could more smoothly (although certainly not perfectly) get through a formal interview or networking event, something important felt lost . . . unrecovered, and missing. Indeed, it was precisely because I was finally able to speak "properly" in Japanese that there seemed to be more distance in my relationships. Part of that is inevitable, since it's difficult to make friends upon moving to any major city; this might be particularly true with Tokyo as a metropolitan area with tens of millions of people, and many foreign tourists. As a result, a foreigner who looks as stereotypically like a *gaijin* as I do becomes totally anonymous, for better or worse.

So while I didn't have children following me around grocery stores shouting *GAIJIN!! GAIJIN!!!!!* at the tops of their lungs anymore, it was perhaps even more shocking when a waiter once took a Japanese menu out of my hands *as I was reading it* to give me the English language version, totally unprompted. It got to be quite difficult, being seen day after day as just another outsider in the mad rush of the Concrete Jungle, where no one seems to have the time to treat each other like the complex human beings they are. I often felt invisible, adrift at sea, and very isolated.

But once a month, I got to escape to Akita for dance lessons . . . and a much-needed vacation from the formal, distant interactions with Tokyoites.

Unlike the formal Japanese one hears so often in Tokyo if not in social situations then over loudspeaker announcements in train stations, department stores, and even in the street, Akita-ben is direct, to the point, and practical—and scarce, not least because there aren't many train stations or department stores in Akita to begin with. Akita-ben is economical, lacking the formality that stifles more standard modes of speaking. Natives to this distant, northern prefecture still use the standard polite verb conjugations of *masu/desu*, but don't get more polite than that unless it's absolutely necessary (sonkeigo is almost laughably out of place there). Some of the older people might not even use *masu/desu* at all, skipping all ornamental language to get right to the point: who are you, and why are you here? And do you need help finding your way?

It's expressive, but not sweet: crisp and bright, yet soft and pearly, like the chirping of chickadees or other birds that don't fly south for the winter. There's a roundness to Akita-ben, with generous use of the emphatic, nasal ん (*n*) that softens intent and obscures the speaker's ego—a mark of beautiful Japanese anywhere. But it's also markedly peppered with unusual, foreign sounds like べ (*be*, pronounced "bay") and ぜ (*ze*, pronounced "zay") rarely heard in standard Japanese due to the influence of the language of the Ainu people, who originally settled, or coexisted with, this northern wilderness.

So since Akita is rural and isolated to begin with, most people not only don't speak "normal" Japanese, they also don't speak any English. Akita-ben is thus rendered the default lingua franca, even if you're a foreigner. From what I can glean, the reasoning flows accordingly: if you're in Akita to begin with, you must know *something* about Japan or speak some kind of Japanese, because you wouldn't have made it up here if you didn't. And if you understand Japanese, then you can probably navigate the way we talk up here. It may be a bit different, but really it's all pretty much the same thing, ain't it?

Well, not exactly, but having it be assumed that you know more of what's going on rather than *less* is a rare treat compared to life in Tokyo.

The irony is that Akita-ben is, in fact, notoriously difficult to understand. Although Kansai-ben probably wins the contest for the most distinctive and easily recognizable dialect in Japan, Akita-ben is known as among the most incomprehensible.[2] And people are proud of that, if saddened by how local young people don't speak it these days since it would limit their job prospects elsewhere, or it's too backward-sounding, or there's never an opportunity to speak it except with your grandparents. And maybe that's true.

But it's also true that cab drivers speak some of the most prolifically incomprehensible Akita-ben out there, along with keepers of noodle shops and inns, as well as musicians and dancers, car rental center clerks, and people you bump into on the street. Which means that, in order to speak Akita-ben, you have to take out the earbuds, get off the smartphone, leave your head, and enter the present moment, where the gentle pace of a Japan past is being lived by increasingly fewer people. When in Akita, do as the Akitans do, right?

It's also true, leaving Husserl, Derrida, and other deconstructionist semantic theorists aside for the moment, that language is so much more than words: it's about what's being communicated in the first place. So while the man who took the menu out of my hands in Tokyo spoke to me in the politest form of Japanese and bowed profusely after I informed him that I wasn't having problems but was simply making up my mind as to what I wanted to eat, he was

---

2 Along with Akita's northern neighbor, Aomori.

communicating a very clear message: you are fundamentally different from me. And while the man in the grocery store in Akita during a white-out blizzard had let me know—without knowing for sure that I was indeed "the researcher" people had heard about—that dance rehearsal had been cancelled (but best of luck anyhow) had used a brusque local dialect without any polite conjugations, formalities, or ornamental bowing, he too communicated a very clear message: you are fundamentally *similar* to me.

Like all good things, one must actively seek Akita-ben to find it. One must *be in Akita* to hear it. And while it can be somewhat hard to find, it is there, in the background, like the song of a chickadee: staccato yet soft, bold yet unpretentious, humble yet strong.

The Celebrity

"Jiru!"

Her voice was deeply emphatic. She had only met me once before at a party in Tokyo in the haunt where I logged the most hours during my "fieldwork": in quotations because, by the end of that year, what had begun as research became my off-duty social life. It was at the party where all the groups and DJs I had followed for nearly a year happened to be doing a show together at my favorite spot, and even though I had since moved to Osaka to finish up my time as a formal researcher, I still showed up three hours and a 14,000 yen bullet train ride later.

It was immediately clear that she was there with one of the night's most notorious performers, the ring-leader of the scene: yep, the Mad Scientist himself. That night, he had replaced his usual "too cool to be here" attitude while hiding in the corner with his hood up and an iPad (and a fat blunt) out with a subtle, nearly mocking pride that this woman was here with him. Although I'd never seen her at a show before, she didn't look shy or tentative like many newcomers do. She blazed with an otherworldly confidence as she danced wildly in front of the speakers, hair flying in all directions while wearing a bizarre white pajama onesie.

The show was good, but around the time the acid tabs were handed out (there was a moment's hesitation when they reached me before ultimately not offering any) I was reminded of the reasons I had chosen to leave Tokyo earlier that summer: the alienation, the extreme polarity between the world out there and the world in the club, how cool everyone tries to be in the Mad City, the nearly blind reverence of a reckless, nearly total abandon of society and self. It had all been too much. At a certain point I could no longer connect with that lifestyle and realized, one day in the springtime, I'd become just another jaded soul drifting half-awake through the Concrete Jungle. Somewhat disappointed on principle but very much relieved in practice that I wasn't included in this inner-sphere ritual of casual hard-drug use, I sipped my consolatory drink on the bar stool, meditating on the year I'd spend in Japan, and ideas of friendship.

Maybe friendship can describe the relationship you have with the people you play music with.

Maybe friendship can describe the relationship you have with the people you do drugs with.

Maybe friendship can describe a relationship where one person cares more than the other, and maybe that's OK.

After the show started to wind down and the trains started running again—and after catching a few z's in my trademark spot behind the soundproof door—I went outside for a breath of fresh air to gather myself before saying goodbye. BOOM: there she was, standing with who was now obviously her boyfriend. He then took it upon himself to introduce me as best as he could in his trademark too-loud stammer, given that he was perpetually fried from dropping way too much acid:

"Hey, hey, this is Jiru. She researches underground music and she's come to practically all our shows, ha. And she also does like, traditional music, it's so crazy. What do you do again, Okinawa? Or . . . Hokkaido? Shit, what was it again? Hey, Jiru, you should really check out Okinawan traditional music. It's so sick. "

It continually struck me as funny that this dude, who prioritized synthesizers and drugs above nearly all else in his life—the person who invited me to a secret mountain rave when I didn't even know him, then ignored me for two solid months after I rejected an awkward sexual advance while still attending his shows, and then suddenly treated me like a chummy pal after declaring, with approving laughter, that I was *atama okashii* [1]—always took it upon himself to explain my research to people. Also interesting is that he paid particular attention not to my work in the underground, but to my interests in traditional music. The absurdity was always compounded by the fact that he could never remember what traditional music I researched, which led to nearly identical stream-of-consciousness conclusions that I should check out Okinawan traditional music if it wasn't what I was already studying. He must have told me to study Okinawan traditional music on at least three separate occasions.

"Haha, thanks . . . um, I actually practice a *bon odori* in Akita prefecture. Nice to meet you. What's your name?"

As she introduced herself, strong eye-contact and mysterious smile communicated an immediate affection; it was clear that she had taken some kind of liking to me. And so, half tipsy and half asleep, I blurted out:

---

1 Sick in the head.

"Hey, I like your outfit. Is that a onesie? Haha!"

Excited by a brief exchange about onesies and shopping in Tokyo, I then pulled out the big guns:

"I love thrift shopping. In America they have these huge junk shops and you can find anything there. See my shorts? I made them from a pair of Lucky brand jeans that I got for three dollars! Do you know Lucky Jeans? They say "Lucky" on the inside of the fly! You can see!"

. . . and that's the story of when I unbuttoned my jeans for a celebrity without knowing it.

. . . the only circumstances under which that could have possibly happened.

I didn't find out she was a celebrity until later that summer, while having lunch with a friend who filled me in. Not only was she a celebrity, my friend explained, but was quickly becoming a full-blown star—she's been in commercials, advertisements, and even appears in gossip magazines. Ah, corporate sponsorship: how you know you've hit the big-time! A part of me was embarrassed recalling the first impression I must have left, but another, bigger part found it to be hilariously perfect.

Later that summer, I sojourned four hours one-way to a sleepy countryside town to say a final goodbye to the same Tokyo crew, who, according to social media and a brief message exchange from the scene's most friendly liaison, had made their way down to western Japan for a show/vacation at a tiny club nestled between a tire shop and a possibly defunct café. After their first trip down there in January, the aforementioned ring-leader had since described it as the "best place in Japan." Slightly regretting making the long trip out to say goodbye to a bunch of people who were probably blacked-out on booze and drugs anyway, I finally arrived . . . and there she was. Her face lit up when I tentatively walked in and, although I had only met her once before, I was happy to see a smiling face among a group that was otherwise totally wasted, passed out in the grass at 4:30 in the afternoon, and coming down from what was very likely a two-day acid bender.

"Jiru!"

Not really feeling the vibe of the party, a suspicion I had long held about this scene solidified: whatever principles about being anti-system and cultivating an authentic identity that these people might have held might very well have been secondary to petty rebellion, and perhaps even some posturing. Where was this all going? What was the actual point? So, only a few minutes after arriving, and having no interest in hearing whatever music was farted out between substance binges, I decided to say goodbye to the cognizant and make my way back to Osaka. The nicest part of that whole excursion was seeing her.

We clicked, you know?

* * *

LATER ON, WE BECAME FRIENDS ON Facebook and even sent each other a few messages. Sure, she didn't mind if I talked about her group in my class back at Cornell; since she had already been formally interviewed by MTV, she didn't need to be interviewed by my little fellowship blog. Definitely, I'd let her know the next time I'm in Japan. Which I did, but either she was in Hokkaido, or in Singapore, or was just too busy, but maybe next time. Yet there never seemed to be the right time, and so I began to realize that this was a classic case of Japanese rejection: just say you're busy enough times, and eventually they'll get the hint and stop contacting you.

So that's what I did.

Maybe being a celebrity means you just don't have the time for or interest in making new friends.

Maybe being a celebrity means that you don't trust people who'd like to be friends with you.

Or maybe being a celebrity means wishing people would actually just be real with you, but if they get a little star struck then you can't be bothered.

Maybe this all makes for a funny story, and maybe some encounters are best left as once-in-a-lifetime.

And maybe that's OK.

Portrait of an (Underground) Artist as a Young Man

UNLIKE TRYING TO MEET UP WITH anyone in the Tokyo scene, DIGITALBOY actually suggested clear dates and showed up on-time—although, to be fair, we did have to reschedule our first meeting due to overly optimistic planning. There was no way either of us could meet the morning after a party, following respective all-nighters.

And that's how it started. It's impossible to parse out the whens and wheres of what has been discussed since then, or to create a clear narrative of it all, from beginning to end. Besides, as a voice he samples on one of his *Boombox Therapy* mixes purrs, "time revolves in circles, and not squares." He has also has explicitly expressed that he "hates words" and prefers to learn and communicate through sound, image, and touch—through feeling.

DIGITALBOY is a talented DJ, producer, and track maker; he's spent significant time in Europe, where he, too, says he felt far more appreciated than he ever has in Japan. Part of that is monetary. Having DJed at major venues in England and Germany—including a rave that took place on an airport runway—he was able to live rather handsomely off of his craft, and in community with like-minded bohemian-types.

Once, DIGITALBOY alleges, he even played a gig with the legendary electronic musician Aphex Twin. After his German artist's visa ran out, though, he had to return to Japan and now regularly falls prey to *utsu*: depression. DIGITALBOY hopes to return to Europe someday, but practical planning and foresight are not his most immediate gifts. This dude is so underground that he's literally *rejected* record deals.

So, in the spirit of how he transmitted this knowledge to me, below is what I came to understand more clearly during my time with DIGITALBOY: the catalyst, the veteran, a nihilistic optimist . . . a man who, despite his blind spots, tries to live fully for his music and art. A man who stubbornly, heroically, and perhaps irrationally refuses to make money by any other means, who rejects standard conditions of "reality," and who clings to his dreams with true grit.

1. Music, art, fashion, and all the other creative sensibilities that a person can explore are linked to form a cohesive aura.

2. Living life according to feeling is of utmost importance; logic often just gets in the way.

3. Feelings are truth.

4. Science can produce misleading results. As Agent K says in *Men in Black*, "A person is smart. People are dumb, panicky, dangerous animals and you know it. Fifteen hundred years ago everybody knew the Earth was the center of the universe. Five hundred years ago, everybody knew the Earth was flat, and fifteen minutes ago, you knew that humans were alone on this planet. Imagine what you'll know tomorrow."

    a. Well, except for the part about aliens . . . probably.

5. Our bodies and mind are one; healing the body heals the mind.

6. The DJ's responsibility to put people back into their bodies through danceable music is nearly sacred— which is why underground music culture exists at the edge of society, and is actively suppressed by the (Japanese) government.[1]

7. Past traumas cloud present understandings of reality, and optimistic possibilities for the future.

8. Capitalism robs people of the ability to live a life based on feeling; it is a system that is immeasurably detrimental to humankind's capacity for happiness.

   a. . . . although, I've come to believe, communism only works on a micro-scale. *Sigh* . . . these are the options, eh?

9. Coincidences have meaning.

10. The most important thing a person can do in their lives is to be fully present: to live exclusively in the here and now by truly feeling feelings, and trusting that everything will work out.

11. A way out of feeling hopelessly disconnected from contemporary times is to find the humor in it all.

12. Fruits and vegetables are a way that the earth communicates with human beings.

13. The process of becoming more in-tune with one's creative self is an irreversible conversion.

---

1 Save for a brief four-year period from 2014–2018 when the ban was lifted to encourage tourism before the Olympics, dancing in public spaces is technically illegal in Japan.

14. One can nurture self-love and self-respect through creative activities.

15. Living for and nurturing one's dreams may very well be our purpose in this life.

16. Art and music are portals to different worlds.

17. "Reality" is an illusion.

18. McDonald's is terrible.[2]

19. Similar to Walt Whitman's declaration in *Leaves of Grass* that we all contain multitudes, we all have many selves, and some of us have selves that are quite divided from one another.

20. Creating is a meditation; it is healing.

21. If artistic output comes from a place of real feeling—if it reflects the artist's process of working through their feelings in the project—then it will have impact on others.

22. To be yourself you must truly *be*, rather than *conceptualize*, who you are.

23. One should not *call* themselves an artist; they should *be* an artist.

24. The nation state is prohibitive, and the world would probably have peace if we could just move around freely without borders.

25. Being 100% anti-system is really difficult, if not impossible.

---

2   But sometimes a Filet-o-Fish really hits the spot when you're homesick in Japan. And let me tell you, McDonald's in Japan is far superior in presentation and taste to the franchises in its nation of origin. Classic Japan, right?

a. Capitalism is a zero-sum game: you cannot truly opt-out, and if you try you will inevitably suckle at the teat of those who are more realistic.

26. If a guy lashes out at you when he's feeling emotionally unstable, it's not your fault, you can't fix him, and you should break up with him immediately.

27. If someone comes onto you really strong in the beginning—like, relentlessly—and then starts putting you down on the regular after you finally let your guard down, this person is bad news and you should run for the hills, in a zig-zag fashion, as fast and as far away from the relationship as you can. Then, do everything in your power to show yourself the love and respect you deserve.

28. Just because you respect someone as an artist doesn't mean you should go out with them.

And, most importantly,

29. If I had a tape recorder for any of our conversations, particularly those first ones when we wandered around the streets of Kyoto and Osaka talking about music, I wouldn't have been able to learn any of this.[3]

---

3   In anthropology, it's often supposed that the best way to give your interlocutors autonomy is to record them, word-for-word. But this inhibits natural conversation, and solidifies the rigid binary between researcher and "subject" that makes interactions clinical, distant, and inorganic. I mentioned this to him on our first real meeting, to which he heartily agreed and let me know that he wouldn't have opened up to me if I'd arrived recorder in-hand. We had this conversation on what turned out to be our first date.

Epilogue

IF THIS WERE A (NOW DELICIOUSLY retro) Choose Your Own Adventure book, with hypotheses instead of story lines, you might have some theoretical inklings about (Japanese) music and society swirling around your head by now.

Any responsible scholar will tell you that evidence creates theory, not the other way around. I venture to say that these twenty tales support certain theoretical stances about capitalism's unfortunate pitfalls, the nature and limits of resistance, and music's overall relationship to society on whole. After all, having these experiences in the first place influenced the conclusions I made in my dissertation. Having thus successfully and safely arrived at the epilogue, now it's your turn to ponder the central question of this book (along with the connections between music in society, in Japan and beyond): Can we absorb theoretical content through stories?

Because I remain wholly uninterested in telling you my own conclusions so much as I am in having you draw your own, I offer the actual abstract and biographical sketch I was required to submit in the few pages of my dissertation. Since they specifically outline my academic argumentation and theoretical leanings as a scholar, they can serve as an apt point of comparison for your own conclusions. Have at it!

(And yes, I really did write that quip about waitressing in the bio. Clearly, I was still kind of a hot mess when I wrote this, without having yet processed all I was feeling about academia. In truth, maybe I never will.)

Liner Notes: Aesthetics of Capitalism and Resistance in Contemporary Japanese Music

Jillian Marshall, Ph.D.
Cornell University 2018

Abstract

THIS DISSERTATION HYPOTHESIZES THAT CAPITALISM CAN be understood as an aesthetic through an examination and comparison of three music life worlds in contemporary Japan: traditional, popular, and underground. Through ethnographic fieldwork-based immersion in each musical world for nearly four years, the research presented here concludes that capitalism's alienating aesthetic is naturally counteracted by aesthetics of community-based resistance, which blur and re-organize the generic boundaries typically associated with these three musics. By conceptualizing capitalism—and socio-economics on whole—as an aesthetic, this dissertation ultimately claims an activist stance, showing by way of these rather dramatic case studies the self-destructive nature of capitalistic enterprise, and its effects on musical styles and performance, as well as community and identity in Japan and beyond.

Biographical Sketch

PRIOR TO UNDERTAKING DOCTORAL STUDIES IN Musicology at Cornell in 2011, Jillian Marshall studied East Asian Languages and Civilizations at the University of Chicago, where she graduated with double honors. Jillian has also studied with other institutions, notably Princeton University through the Princeton in Beijing Program (PiB, 2007), and Columbia University through the Kyoto Consortium of Japanese Studies at Dōshisha University (KCJS, 2012). Her interest in the music of Japan was piqued during her initial two-year tenure in the country, when she worked as a middle school English teacher in a rural fishing village. Other research interests include Marxism, activist scholarship, and the broader relationship between music and society, particularly in societies of drastic upheaval (such as China, the former USSR, and Mexico). In addition to her work as a teacher, Jillian is a dancer, musician, and writer, with aspirations to cultivate these vocational possibilities to their fullest potential. She also has been happily working as a waitress since her time at Cornell.[1]

---

1 Happy for a while, anyway. While still in school and immediately after, when I was working as an adjunct professor, waitressing was a fun escape where I could earn money without having to crawl inside the nether reaches of my brain. However, the "Let's Be A Waitress and See What Happens" experiment ended up forming the basis for my second book.

Acknowledgements

FIRST AND FOREMOST, I COULDN'T HAVE done this without the support of my family. Mom, your unfettered belief in my path keeps me optimistic even when the odds seem grim; Dad, you give me courage to live life MY way, no matter what everyone else is doing; Brooke, you keep the bar high, and journeying toward something greater as life-long collaborators is my biggest inspiration. Special thanks during the Padma and 725 days. My gratitude also goes out to Aunt Jo-Ann and Uncle Dean for back-to-school shopping, as well as everyone else in the family on both sides (Lee, Gramma + Grampa, Aunt Skeet, Aunt Claire, Richard + Sara, Robin, Doug, and my sweet pal Patty McTavish). Thank you.

Thank you to Heidi, Ernie, and Alexis for coming to my PhD death march of a graduation and/or staying up late with Brooke and me during our formative years, actually listening to our ideas and making us feel empowered, validated, and heard.

I extend deep gratitude to my professors over the years, particularly Roger Moseley, Steven Pond and Naoki Sakai, as well as Brett deBary, Neal Zaslaw, James Webster, Aaron Fox, Michael Raine, Paja Faudree, Norma Field, Alejandro Madrid, and Paul Merrill. Xièxiè to the Chinese Department at UChicago!

Huge thank you to the brilliant graduate students (/war buddies) at Cornell whom I have the privilege to call both colleagues and friends. That's Erica Levenson, Annalise Smith, Jordan Musser, Mackenzie Pierce, Nicco Athens, Shin Hwang, Michael Small, and especially my dissertation writing buddy Matthew Hall—who told me I should publish this as "a real book that, you know, people might actually read." Big ups to all of my amazing undergraduate students at Cornell; teaching you all was the highlight of the whole gig. #3111 #Z2JP

My heartfelt thanks goes out to all of my teachers growing up in Vermont, especially Ms. Scott, Ms. B-C, Mrs. and Mr. Pigeon, Mrs. Larose, and my English teacher Ms. Chaput. Your creativity, attention, and care made all the difference. Thank you, John Baxter.

Thanks to the folks at Fulbright Japan, who were extra supportive of my research and encouraged me to speak about it.

Without exaggeration, I couldn't have made it through the grim final stretch at Cornell without the family at Hai Hong Restaurant in Ithaca. Helen, Khon, and Eddie Quach, Li Wong, Peipei Chang, Soth Soeun, Thomas Lu, and Li Fang: thank you for feeding me, and giving me vital experience for the next chapter of my life—all puns intended, since that's my second book! HUGE thanks to the brilliant Anne Hamilton and Walter Chong: my Ithaca guardian angels.

Thank you to my friends at UChicago, who are some of the most intelligent and interesting people I'll ever met—especially Bonnie Li and Dave MacDonald, who were key players on the journeys to China, and Brian Leahy, who also found himself at Cornell (and at the nexus of industry and academia). Special thanks for all those breakfasts at Hal's.

Arigatou gozaimasu to my friends in Japan. Lily: where to even start? Forever classified though they shall remain, our gchats during the JET years constituted my original field notes on Japanese society. If it weren't for you, I wouldn't have had the ultimate travel buddy (death marches aside) and would still be listening to clown music alone in my house. Fukushima Marine Day 2022? (Also: Sup Yoshi?) Charlotte: our trip in Akita was a revelation, as is every encounter with you. Thank you for introducing a world to me where I felt at home—the import of which you understand more than most. *Domo arigatou gozaimasu* to Noguchi Sensei, as well as Kawasaki Tazuko, Oka Tomofumi, the Miyamoto Family, Maegawa Sensei down in Awaji Island. Minatsu, Cain, Paul, Dayna, and the family at G. Elm: thank you for those wild times at WAVE karaoke . . .

Then there are the musicians and partygoers who made this whole thing possible, both in the underground and in the old world. Kokoro kara arigatou Kaori-chan, Tsubitto-san, Sachiko-san, Shindo-kun, Tomo, Batico, Maikii, Nanae, Napalm-san, Hayato, Rimitossu, Yusuke, Maririn, Mitsuki, Yae, Nakahara-san, Miso-chan and Mae-chan, and yes, Masayuki. Sato-san, Numakura-san, Pat, Yano-san, thank you. Yumiko-san, our cute weekly lunches (and Akita connection!) made the Concrete Jungle a little more sweet.

I am so grateful for my New York City circle, especially the goddess herself Satya Celeste, the folks at SSHH, Greta Hawkins, Cait Goodman + Nathan Weger—Bushwick Royalty, Winslow "Pop Dod" Cavanaugh, and Jenny Akchin. You push me to self-actualize because you push yourselves, and I have the strength to blossom into a writer because of that. THANK YOU to the wonderful folks at Three Rooms Press, especially Mary—*Editor Extraordinaire*—who was instrumental in making this dream of mine a reality. And last: super special thanks to Justin, whose presence in my life is as soothing as a sitting on a mossy boulder in a stream in the woods, and without whom I wouldn't have had the focus to do any of what I'm—we're—doing.

<3
Onward and upward!

RECENT AND FORTHCOMING BOOKS FROM THREE ROOMS PRESS

FICTION

Lucy Jane Bledsoe
No Stopping Us Now

Rishab Borah
The Door to Inferna

Meagan Brothers
Weird Girl and What's His Name

Christopher Chambers
Scavenger
Standalone

Ebele Chizea
Aquarian Dawn

Ron Dakron
Hello Devilfish!

Robert Duncan
Loudmouth

Michael T. Fournier
Hidden Wheel
Swing State

Aaron Hamburger
Nirvana Is Here

William Least Heat-Moon
Celestial Mechanics

Aimee Herman
Everything Grows

Kelly Ann Jacobson
Tink and Wendy

Jethro K. Lieberman
Everything Is Jake

Eamon Loingsigh
Light of the Diddicoy
Exile on Bridge Street

John Marshall
The Greenfather

Aram Saroyan
Still Night in L.A.

Robert Silverberg
The Face of the Waters

Stephen Spotte
Animal Wrongs

Richard Vetere
The Writers Afterlife
Champagne and Cocaine

Julia Watts
Quiver
Needlework

Gina Yates
Narcissus Nobody

MEMOIR & BIOGRAPHY

Nassrine Azimi and Michel Wasserman
Last Boat to Yokohama: The Life and Legacy of Beate Sirota Gordon

William S. Burroughs & Allen Ginsberg
Don't Hide the Madness:
William S. Burroughs in Conversation with Allen Ginsberg
edited by Steven Taylor

James Carr
BAD: The Autobiography of James Carr

Judy Gumbo
Yippie Girl: Exploits in Protest and Defeating the FBI

Judith Malina
Full Moon Stages:
Personal Notes from 50 Years of The Living Theatre

Phil Marcade
Punk Avenue: Inside the New York City Underground, 1972–1982

Jillian Marshall
Japanthem: Counter-Cultural Experiences; Cross-Cultural Remixes

Alvin Orloff
Disasterama! Adventures in the Queer Underground 1977–1997

Nicca Ray
Ray by Ray: A Daughter's Take on the Legend of Nicholas Ray

Stephen Spotte
My Watery Self:
Memoirs of a Marine Scientist

PHOTOGRAPHY-MEMOIR

Mike Watt
On & Off Bass

SHORT STORY ANTHOLOGIES

SINGLE AUTHOR

The Alien Archives: Stories
by Robert Silverberg

First-Person Singularities: Stories
by Robert Silverberg
with an introduction by John Scalzi

Tales from the Eternal Café: Stories
by Janet Hamill, with an introduction
by Patti Smith

Time and Time Again:
Sixteen Trips in Time
by Robert Silverberg

Voyagers:
Twelve Journeys in Space and Time
by Robert Silverberg

MULTI-AUTHOR

Crime + Music: Twenty Stories of Music-Themed Noir
edited by Jim Fusilli

Dark City Lights: New York Stories
edited by Lawrence Block

The Faking of the President: Twenty Stories of White House Noir
edited by Peter Carlaftes

Florida Happens:
Bouchercon 2018 Anthology
edited by Greg Herren

Have a NYC I, II & III:
New York Short Stories;
edited by Peter Carlaftes
& Kat Georges

Songs of My Selfie:
An Anthology of Millennial Stories
edited by Constance Renfrow

The Obama Inheritance:
15 Stories of Conspiracy Noir
edited by Gary Phillips

This Way to the End Times:
Classic and New Stories of the Apocalypse
edited by Robert Silverberg

MIXED MEDIA

John S. Paul
Sign Language: A Painter's Notebook
(photography, poetry and prose)

DADA

Maintenant: A Journal of Contemporary Dada Writing & Art
(Annual, since 2008)

HUMOR

Peter Carlaftes
A Year on Facebook

FILM & PLAYS

Israel Horovitz
My Old Lady: Complete Stage Play and Screenplay with an Essay on Adaptation

Peter Carlaftes
Triumph For Rent (3 Plays)
Teatrophy (3 More Plays)

Kat Georges
Three Somebodies: Plays about Notorious Dissidents

TRANSLATIONS

Thomas Bernhard
On Earth and in Hell
(poems of Thomas Bernhard with English translations by Peter Waugh)

Patrizia Gattaceca
Isula d'Anima / Soul Island
(poems by the author in Corsican with English translations)

César Vallejo | Gerard Malanga
Malanga Chasing Vallejo
(selected poems of César Vallejo with English translations and additional notes by Gerard Malanga)

George Wallace
EOS: Abductor of Men
(selected poems in Greek & English)

ESSAYS

Richard Katrovas
Raising Girls in Bohemia:
Meditations of an American Father

Far Away From Close to Home
Vanessa Baden Kelly

Womentality: Thirteen Empowering Stories by Everyday Women Who Said Goodbye to the Workplace and Hello to Their Lives
edited by Erin Wildermuth

POETRY COLLECTIONS

Hala Alyan
Atrium

Peter Carlaftes
DrunkYard Dog
I Fold with the Hand I Was Dealt

Thomas Fucaloro
It Starts from the Belly and Blooms

Kat Georges
Our Lady of the Hunger

Robert Gibbons
Close to the Tree

Israel Horovitz
Heaven and Other Poems

David Lawton
Sharp Blue Stream

Jane LeCroy
Signature Play

Philip Meersman
This Is Belgian Chocolate

Jane Ormerod
Recreational Vehicles on Fire
Welcome to the Museum of Cattle

Lisa Panepinto
On This Borrowed Bike

George Wallace
Poppin' Johnny

Three Rooms Press | New York, NY | Current Catalog: www.threeroomspress.com
Three Rooms Press books are distributed by Publishers Group West: www.pgw.com